MCKENZIE'S FIGHTING FIFTH

Questionnaires of Veterans of the 5th Tennessee Cavalry Regiment Confederate States of America

Transcribed by
Carl Campbell

Rhea County Historical and
Genealogical Society

Heritage Books
2024

HERITAGE BOOKS
AN IMPRINT OF HERITAGE BOOKS, INC.

Books, CDs, and more—Worldwide

For our listing of thousands of titles see our website
at
www.HeritageBooks.com

A Facsimile Reprint
Published 2024 by
HERITAGE BOOKS, INC.
Publishing Division
5810 Ruatan Street
Berwyn Heights, MD 20740

Copyright © 1999 Rhea County Historical
and Genealogical Society

— Publisher's Notice —
In reprints such as this, it is often not possible to remove
blemishes from the original. We feel the contents of this
book warrant its reissue despite these blemishes and
hope you will agree and read it with pleasure.

International Standard Book Number
Paperbound: 978-0-7884-8717-0

FOREWORD

Dr. Gus Dyer, State Archivist, sent questionnaires in 1914 and 1915 to all known living Tennessee Civil War Veterans, stating that his purpose was to collect information needed to produce a true history of the Old South. In 1920, John Trotwood Moore, Director of the Tennessee Historical Committee, followed up with a revised form of the same questionnaire. Tennessee Confederate veterans returned 1,466 questionnairs and Federal veterans 115.

The quality of the responses varies widely; some veterans gave little information, others included attachments covering many pages of narrative about their experiences in the war. Some responses were crudely written in pencil or ink and are barely legible, others were neatly typewritten. For many of the veterans the war was so far in the past the events had become a chaotic jumble in their memories while others accurately recalled the exact sequence of their experiences and details of their service. As a consequence the material, while always interesting, often cannot be relied upon to be historically accurate.

In February 1985, the *Journal of Southern History* published an article by Fred Arthur Bailey, associate professor of history at Abilene Christian University, entitled "Class and Tennessee's Confederate Generations" (Vol. LI, No. 1, pp. 31-60) based upon the responses to these questionnaires. The same year, the Southern Historical Press, Easley, South Carolina, published in five volumes a transcription of the entire collection — ***Tennessee Civil War Veterans' Questionnaires*** — edited by Colleen Morse (Mrs. O.L.) Elliott and Louise Armstrong (Mrs. R.L.) Moxley. In 1987, Bailey's article was expanded to book length and published by the North Carolina Press under the same title as the earliest article.

Questionnaires were completed by veterans or family members for twenty of the 5th (McKenzie's) Tennessee Cavalry Regiment, C. S. A. More than half of these are veterans who lived in the counties of Rhea, Meigs, and Bradley, and they were no doubt under the influence and urging of W.G. Allen whose unedited papers contain a letter from John Trotwood Moore dated February 10, 1920, which states, "I have added your name to our Collaborating Committee for your county. At the proper time you will be formally notified by Governor Roberts."

The transcriptions presented here contain twenty-two questionnaires from members of the 5th Regiment (William Godsey and L.M. King returned both forms). While the spelling is unaltered, the responses have been punctuated and paragraphed to enhance readability. A brief introduction for each veteran includes service records, abstracted from National Archive files. End notes have been added to clarify or correct some of the answers, principally those of William G. Allen. An abbreviated form of each question in italics precedes each response to give a context, and an appendix contains the full text of both questionnaires, Form A being the earlier, sent in 1914 and 1915. An index references the veterans' responses.

Carl E. Campbell
715 Brookfield Avenue
Chattanooga, Tennessee

April 1997

CONTENTS

ALLEN, WILLIAM GIBBS	1
Form A	3
BLEVINS, WILLIAM F.	31
Form A	32
CHARLTON, JOSEPH EDWARD	36
Form B	37
COOLEY, JOHN FRANKLIN	41
Form A	42
CRAWFORD, JOHN TYLER	46
Form B	47
DAVIS, WILLIAM OWEN	52
Form B	53
DUCKWORTH, D. FRANK	56
Form A	57
GODSEY, WILLIAM CLENTON	61
Form A	62
Form B	66
GRIFFITH, ISAAC	70
Form A	71
GUFFEE, ANDY WHITE	77
Form A	78
HUNTER, PLEASANT EAVES	81
Form A	82
JONES, MARTIN V.	86
Form B	87
KING, LUKE M. C.	90
Form A	91
Form B	95
McKENZIE, JEREMIAH M.	98
Form B	99
MOORE, EBENEZER MELVIN PATTEN	103
Form B	104
SEHON, JOHN F.	107
Form B	108
WHITSON, WILLIAM MANING	112
Form B	113
WOLFE, JOHN	116
Form A	117
WOOD, TOLIVER	120
Form B	121
WOODY, WILLIAM JEFFERSON	124
Form B	125
NOTES	129
FORM A TEXT	132
FORM B TEXT	135
INDEX	138

WILLIAM GIBBS ALLEN

In the early 1900's, William Gibbs Allen wrote at great length about his service with McKenzie's 5th Regiment. A series of articles was published in the *Dayton Herald* in 1911, 1912, and 1918, and several essays can be found in the *Confederate Veteran*. There is evidence that he submitted articles to other publications. Before his death he sent to John Trotwood Moore a box of manuscripts, newspaper clippings, and correspondence which is in the Tennessee State Archives. The Rhea County Historical and Genealogical Society also has several hundred pages of clippings and manuscripts covering early Rhea County history as well as Civil War events. These will in due time be edited for publication.

In submitting his response to his veteran's questionnaire, Allen attached many pages which were filed in the Archives apart from the printed form. These have been included here in the appropriate places so that his comments are restored to their original state.

Allen's responses are sometimes difficult to evaluate because there are many documentable errors of fact which create doubt about other statements which cannot be easily corroborated. While some discrepancies might be attributable to a failing memory, others appear to be more or less deliberate flights of fancy.

As his service record shows, Allen enlisted on April 5, 1862, three months after the 1st (Rogers') Tennessee Cavalry Regiment was organized. He sometimes refers to the unit in its early days as the 2nd Regiment but always incorrectly gives the date of March instead of December 1862 as the date the 5th Regiment was organized.

He was absent from the regiment on sick leave three months from November 1, 1862 to February 12, 1863; he was absent from September 19 to December 2, 1863, having been wounded at Chickamauga, and missed Wheeler's first Tennessee raid; he was absent three months from August 14 to early November, 1864, having been separated from the regiment during Wheeler's second Tennessee raid.

Allen died November 27, 1924, at the home of his daughter in Chattanooga, Tennessee, in the eighty-ninth year. He was buried beside his wife in Buttram Cemetery in Dayton, Rhea County, Tennessee.

ALLEN, WILLIAM G.; 2Lt (D) 5th (McKenzie's) Tennessee Cavaley Regiment

Residence: Washington, Rhea County
Enlisted: April 5, 1862 at Kingston by J.F. Rogers for 12 months
Age: 26 on March 11, 1864 roll
Paroled: May 3, 1865 at Charlotte, North Carolina

Muster Rolls

Present	1862 Feb 14 - Apr 30	(I - 1st Regt)
Present	1862 May - June	(I - 1st Regt)

Elected 2nd Lt May 24, 1862

Present	1862 Jul - Aug	(D - 2nd Bn)
Present	1862 Sep - Oct	(D - 2nd Bn)
Absent	1862 Nov - Dec	(D - 5th Regt)

Sick since November 1, 1862 by surgeon's certificate

Present	1863 Jan - Feb	(D - 5th Regt)

(signed roll as commanding)

Present	1864 Mar 11	(D - 5th Regt)
Present	1863 Mar - Apr	(D - 5th Regt)
Present	1864 Nov - Dec	(D - 5th Regt)

Appointed Acting Adjutant April 1, 1864

1863 Nov 3

An April 27, 1864 Hickory Station, North Carolina, abstract of payments by George W. Allen, Captain and AQM 3rd Tennessee Volunteers, shows payment on November 3, 1863 $360.00 to W.G. Allen for period from July 1, 1863 to October 31, 1863

1863 Dec 31

Certificate of payment W. G. Allen drew from George W. Allen $870.00 in payment for 9 months. January 1 to March 31, 1864: 3 months at $90 = $270. April 1 to September 30, 1864: 6 months at $100 = $600.

1864 Jan 17

Cave Springs, Georgia. Lt. Allen drew forage for 14 horses for two days.

QUESTIONNAIRE A
January 1922

1. *Name and Address:*
   William Gibbs Allen, 651 South Market St., Dayton, Tenn.

2. *Current age:*
   I have passed my 86th birthday. I am a teetotaler on whiskey and tobacco.

3. *State and county of birth:*
   At Larkinsville, Jackson County, Alabama.

4. *Where living when enlisted as Confederate or Federal:*
   Confederate. I was living in Washington, Rhea County, Tennessee, when I enlisted.

5. *Occupation before the war:*
   I was a merchant and farmer.

6. *Occupation of your father:*
   Farmer.

7. *Value of property you owned:*
   I owned a small farm, value of property about two thousand dollars. I was Trustee of Rhea County and Deputy Register. Held a small stock of goods. I resigned both and went into Captain John George Morgan Montgomery's Bradley County Cavalry Company.

8. *Slaves owned, if any:*
   None.

9. *Land your parents owned:*
   211.

10. *Value of parents' property at onset of war:*
    Land $2,500. Household goods, horses, and cattle about $1,500.

11. *Kind of house your parents owned:*
    One large log house. Later a two story frame with porch in front, 2 rooms down and 2 upstairs.

12. *What kind of work you did as boy and young man:*
    I was ten years old when War came between America and Mexico. Father and Uncle Abner Frazier had a 4 horse crop rented on Tennessee River bottoms. Uncle Abner and A. Richardson volunteered and left father the 4 horse crop to tend. I had made a hand with hoe, now I made a plough hand.

13. *Kind of work your father and mother did:*
    Father did all kind of work on the leased land. We boys (for their was 7 boys and one girl) grubbed, burnt brush. Mother cooked, washed, patched, made tow cloth. When a web of cloth

was wove she made up long tow shorts. I helped her. She would card a pile of reels and I would spin till bed time. I helped to clear the loom and fill the reel and weave the cloth at night.

14. *Servants your parents kept, if any:*
No. Sometimes Father would hire help to work on the farm.

15. *Was honest toil respected in your community:*
Our neighborhood considered a lazy man that would not work as worthless as mean --?-- [scum?]. Day labor was respectable in rich and poor families.

16. *Did white men engage in toil:*
Yes. Rich and poor alike.

17. *Did white men idle while others worked.*
Their was but few men that would not work and the few their was was not respected and hated by rich and poor. Mothers the girls of that day would not keep company with such dudes [sic].

18. *Did slave owners mingle or feel themselves better:*
I married into a slave owner family. My wife, Miss Mary E. Thomison, associated with daughters of slave owners. My wife had one beau who owned 40 slaves and one who had 10 slaves. My best man had no slaves. My wife's best young lade had 30. At our wedding there was 30 invited guests. Rich and poor were invited.

19. *At public gatherings did slave owners mingle freely:*
At church gatherings of all kinds you could not tell by dress or groups, for all classes were respected save the lazy, worthless fellow. At our social parties the poor boy would have as his pardner the rich girl.

In the 1840's and 1850's it was common for a farmer, renter, or land owner to invite his neighbors, rich and poor, to help raise a log house or barn. All would respond. I have seen a slave owner on one corner of a log barn or house, a negro on the other. The man who could make the best notch and keep the straightest corner was chosen and others would carry and pass the log to the corner men. I have seen slave owners and very poor men on each side of a heavy log when a farmer wanted to roll his logs into heaps to be burned.

In 1848 my father had 60 or 70 acres of Tennessee River bottom in corn. In May, the fence caught fire. The fence was through woods in the river hill above the tide of the Tennessee River. One Sunday the neighborhood was at church at old Gum Springs. A runner came and announced that a mile or more of the fence that enclosed our corn crop had been burned. Esqr. Hooper called for all classes to meet him at John Campbell's gate next morning at 7 o'clock with axe, wedge, and maul.

They came, slave owners and slave, side by side. The fence row was through timbered land. Esqr. Hooper laid off section men to cut the timber; men to split the rails, men to build fence and boys to carry water. Before sunset the fence was up. Father was happy, for the neighbors would not have a cent. Good will of all neighbors, slave holders and non slave holders.

20. *Were slave owners and non-owners antagonistic:*
Not so much then as [now] in politics. My father wanted me to marry into a Democrat family but I chose the daughter of a Whig family and we was raised into [within two] miles of [one] another and went to a three months school together once.

21. *Did owning slaves give a political advantage:*
It did not, as you can see from appended sheet [next paragraph], neither in marriage relations. It was character and work that made the man.

In 1859, I was a candidate for Trustee. My opponent was a slave owner, had served the county 6 years, had a good record. My Democratic friends prevailed on me to make the race. I had no money and he had probably $500 (five hundred dollars). Dr. John Hoyal, a strenuous Democrat, and Mr. [W.] E. Colville, a strenuous Whig and a know-nothing, was both slave owners and both supporting me. I rode from house to house to see each voter and the campaign did not cost me 4 dollars. Vote buying had not begun then. Six of Valentine and Ann Frazier Allen's children lived to be grown and all married into slave owning families except Judge V. C. Allen. The Abolition Party had not invaded the land in those days.

22. *Were opportunities good for a poor young man:*
It was honesty and willingness to work was all that was required. Character made the man, not negroes or money.

23. *Did slave owners encourage or discourage poor young men:*
A slave holder & a Whig once hired me to work in his store. I had just made & hauled and built into a fence 5,000 fence rails. Hauled them with a yoke of oxen. Hired me at $12.50 per month to work in his store. At the end of 6 months I was half owner on a credit extended to me.

24. *Kind of school you attended:*
A subscription school two months in Mississaippi, a subscription school in Washington. In 1845 father boarded me and paid $3.00 for my tuition: 3 months at Gum Springs, 3 months at Black Jack School. Log houses, puncheon floors, 4 leg benches.

25. *How long did you go to school:*
Some fifteen and a half months.

26. *How far was it to the nearest school:*
Two miles.

27. *What schools operated in your neighborhood:*
None but subscription schools.

28. *Was the school public or private:*
Public. All white children went, rich and poor, that could pay $1.00 per month.

29. *How many months a year did it run:*
From 1 - 1/2 to 3 months.

30. *Did boys and girls attend regularly:*
All was glad to go.

31. *Was the teacher a man or a woman:*
All were men.

32. *Year and month you enlisted:*
In Confederate March 1st 1861. Would of [gone] in sooner if it had [not] been for my family and my office.

33. *Your Regiment: Members of your company:*
Fifth Tenn. Cavalry, Col. George W. McKenzie, Co. D. First Captain John George Morgan Montgomery's Bradley County Company. I had made an infantry company for Col. J. W. Gillespie's 43rd Regiment but owing to my family and my Trustees office, I could not leave till after settlement and the confinement of my wife. When I went to Knoxville, I found Col. Gillespie's Regiment full and he took me to Col. James T. --?-- [Hayes?]. I found him drunk and I would not serve under him.

I came home and dismissed my men. I and my 17 year old brother, V. C. Allen, mounted our horses and rode to Kingston with the intention of joining Capt. G. W. McKenzie's regiment company from Meigs County. We decided to join Capt. J. G. M. Montgomery's Bradley County Company. Brother and I joined as privates. The Bradley County company was large and intelligent.

When the 5th Regiment was organized, Capt. McKenzie was elected Colonel and Capt. Montgomery, Lieutenant Colonel and Capt. Blackwell of Hamilton County, Major. Lt. Col. Montgomery was a down East Yankee from New York who came south in 1856, settled in Chattanooga for two years then moved to Cleveland. He was a good fighter and a noble gentleman. On organization of the 5th Tennessee Cavalry, Lieutenant R. F. Sloan was made Adjutant, I was elected 3rd Lieutenant, Lt. A. W. Beagles, who deserted and went to Canada, was Captain. J. Alex Davis became 1st Lieutenant and commanded Company D of the 5th till the surrender at Charlotte April 27th, 1865.

In August 1862, R. F. Sloan was severely wounded.[1] He was never able from then for duty in field service. September 20th 1862, Col. McKenzie made me Adjutant of the 5th Tennessee Cavalry[2] and I served as such till surrender at Charlotte, N.C., April 27th 1865.

Gen. Joseph Wheeler promoted me to Major on Account of gallantry in leading three charges made on the Pickett Mill and Powder Springs Road. Two of Sherman's Corps had been dispatched to turn Johnston's right. While he was fighting the New Hope or Dallas battle two small brigades of Cavalry (Ashby's Tennessee and Allen's Alabama) held their two corps for four hours till Johnston sent Pat Cleburne to reinforce us. We was out of ammunition. The 5th Tennessee Cavalry lost 143 out of 500 effective men, lost more than in the bloody battle of Chickamauga. Col. McKenzie was sick and Lt. Col. Montgomery was wounded at Tilton, Georgia and we had no major.

On June 14th 1864, Col. McKenzie returned for duty and had an order read promoting me to Major [3]. I told him I would not serve. I had called the boys so often and they had always responded and followed when I called. I would not leave them till the end came and I surrendered as their adjutant at North Carolina.

34. *After enlistment where was your company sent:*
To Brimstone, Ky.,[4] then to London, Ky. to Camp Dick Roberson, to Danville, Ky. At Dick Roberson we burned a large supply of bacon and several wagons under Gen. John Pegram.

35. *How long before your first battle:*
Two weeks at Brimstone, Kentucky, and Barberville, Ky. At Goose Creek I had a horse shot by bushwhackers.

36. *Your first battle:*
At Williamsburg, Kentucky we fought the Fifth Ohio. Lost a Lt. of Co. G, Horner[5], and 11 detailed men.

37. *Your experience in the war:*
We furnished our own horses and arms. Our arms was a shotgun or Colts pistol. Sometimes an old flintlock rifle. Our saddels poor. We soon captured better guns and saddels. The western horse was no good to a Tennessee or Kentucky cavalry man. They wanted medium sized horses, keen and active. We had no tents. The rich and Government furnished a blanket apiece for each man. The heavens was our covers, rain or shine, by day or night in cold or heat.

In March 1863, Gen. John Pegram went into Kentucky and gathered a great number of beef cattle.[6] When near Summersett, Kentucky, the Federals pressed Pegram so close he formed a line of battle and sent Capt. Kolb's Battery to the front. Kolb's Battery soon drove the Yankees back. Kolb followed and whipped the fight.

Gen. Pegram was a West Point officer. He ordered a court martial by Capt. A. L. Mimms of Co. F of the 5th Tennessee, Capt. Jakes of Scott's 1st Louisiana Tigers, and your humble servant. We took the proof and found that Capt. Kolb had disobeyed orders, but that he had whipped the enemy and that was what we was out for.

After the war Mimms moved to Nashville and established the Mimms' School, some five miles out of Nashville, and ran for Governor of Tennessee twice on the Green Back Party. Capt. Kolb ran for Governor of Alabama twice. Neither was elected. Kolb was a brave man. Mimms was an honorable, clean Presbyterian.

In March 1863 Gen. Pegram made a raid into Kentucky. We struck the enemy at London and met Pegram at Camp Dick Roberson. Here one of the most spectacular fights began. Near Danville we encountered some 3,000 (three thousand) Federals. The night was dark and rain falling. We got mixed up. Yankees were asking who you was, Rebs asking Yankees who they were. Our brigade was small but we charged every thing we met and when day came Gen. Fry and his 3,000 men were moving rapidly for Fort Nelson. There were 3,000 Yankees there.

Here Pegram mounted gun cannons along his line and detailed 240 men of the 16th Tennessee Battalion, Col. J. R. Neal, to gallop in sight of the Yankees, pass under a hill around to where they started, and pass in front again. Asa Johnson, who now lives in the next block to me, was one of the galloping party and says he was nearly galloped out.[7] The balance of Pegram's brigade gathered cattle all over that bluegrass section and succeeded in driving out many head for use of the Confederacy.

Col. Allston took command of Scott's 1st Louisiana, Ashby's 2nd Tennessee, McKenzie's 5th Tennessee and Hart's 6th Georgia and starved Gen. Morgan out of Cumberland Gap. We lived on green corn, had no salt, fed our horses 13 stalks a day, ate 13 ears each day for two weeks. Here I got my second horse shot.

When Morgan evacuated the Gap [8] we followed. At Goose Creek I got my third horse wounded. We fought at Crab Orchard, Stanton, Big Hill, and Stanford. At Richmond we had a hard fight. At Paris and at Lawrenceburg we fought on the 6th of October. We were ordered to Harrodsburg on the 7th. We were ordered to Gen. Bragg's right at Perryville. On the 8th in a charge made by Gen. Wharton on Buell's 20 cannons through an open field with a cross fire on us of 20 pieces of artillery, we suffered a heavy loss.

Col. Allston had fallen and Col. McKenzie took command of our brigade and we was the rear guard to Sycamore Shoals in Tennessee. After Allston was killed, Col. John S. Scott was our brigade commander till after the battle of Chickamauga, 19th September 1863.

When Gen. John H. Morgan invaded Ohio, our brigade was sent into Kentucky to draw off as many troops as possible from pursuit of Morgan.[9] We entered by way and through Crab Orchard and had our usual fight along this route, it being our fourth invasion, and our fourth fight at Big Hill, Stanton, and Sanford. At Richmond we had a very heavy fight, hand to hand and here I got my first gun shot in my left arm, and my shoulder knocked with a gun so I could not use my right arm for two weeks. Had my horse killed from under me.

Col. Scott was drunk. He made Shelby Williams, his adjutant, write an order for me to take 100 men of the 5th Tennessee and go to Paris that night and burn the railroad trestle on the Maysville Railroad. I protested but he made the order. The next day at daylight I encountered a heavy force, lost two men killed and a cannon ball killed another horse for me and I was cut off from the Lexington and Richmond Pike in the woods and had no pilot all night. Late next evening I got to our regiment in line of battle.

Soon a heavy force appeared in Scott's rear and his surrender was ordered by Gen. Burnsides. Scott asked for terms. Burnsides said unconditional surrender. This parley was kept up till 10 o'clock at night when the 5th Tennessee was ordered to cut our way out on Winchester Pike, which we did.

Scott and his artillery moved south and crossed the Kentucky River while Burnsides and Buell was giving chase to the 5th Tennessee. We was in Kentucky 12 days and came out over the roughest road this side of the Rocky Mountains, passing through Hazzard, county site of Hazzard County, into Virginia. We had lost 43 men and many horses, nearly all of the horses barefooted and one half of our men bareheaded. Scott made good with his battery and Gen. Sander's battery that we captured in the Richmond battle when we captured nearly all of his Brigade. I lost 3 horses on this trip, two killed from under me, one with a foot so inflamed from being barefooted his hoofs came off.

In April I was ordered to take 100 men and proceed to London, Kentucky by way of Williamsburg and destroy a large amount of bacon and other army supplies. The ferry boat was small. I sent Lt. Horner of Co. G forward with the first ten men that crossed the river to the X roads from Williamsburg to London and Barboursville to Summerset to wait till I got up with the 90 men. Horner went beyond the cross roads and was led into a trap in a gulch. Horner and the ten men were murdered in this trap![10] When I came I could not see a man.

I lined up my men, cut 5 off of the right and ordered them to advance on the bluff, the same orders given to the left. When they started, the Yankees under cover opened fire on our line, shot my horse so I had to leave him. We pressed on. It proved to be the 5th Ohio Regiment. We captured one lieutenant, burnt much supplies. It was a costly trip. Lt. Horner was a good brave officer.

I fought the Lawrenceburg battle and the Perryville battle with typhoid fever and brought up the rear of Bragg's army from Perryville to Cumberland Gap. On 24th of October 1862, there fell a 4 inch snow. We had no tents. Col. McKenzie could not get a furlough for me.[11] I took a boy who had left home and come to me, John Loyd, and he helped me up and down for three days till I got to Washington.[12] I was unconscious for 3 weeks or more. I pulled through and found my regiment at Maryville on the 12th of February 1863.

Col. McKenzie had orders for me to take 100 men and go to Murphy, N.C. and disperse one Bryson who had burned the Murphy jail and some of the best buildings in the town.[13] Bryson learned I was coming. He moved down the Hiwassee River some 7 miles and forted on a high point with some 300 men. We routed him, killed 7 of his men, and returned to Maryville without the loss of a man. Had three horses shot by bushwhackers.

In March we invaded Kentucky again. Destroyed bacon and flour at Camp Dick Roberson, fought Col. Wm. Clift at Rock Castle. Clift fell back, we did not follow. The Sander's raid came.[14] They attempted to burn the railroad bridges from Charleston on the Hiwassee River to Bulls Gap. Col. Ashby's 2nd Tennessee lost one of his best officers while chasing the raiders, Lieutenant Gibbs. Scott, Ashby and McKenzie could not enduce them into battle. Their leaders knew all the roads and by paths to the mountain passes.

In an engagement at Summersett, Kentucky, Col. Ashby was shot in the heel, and fought the war through with one crutch and was murdered on Gay Street, Knoxville, one E. S. Camp shooting him in the back while he was on crutches crossing the steet. After the war a rebel had no protection. Brownlow as good as told his militia he would protect them in their murders of rebels.

I had fought at every cross roads from Summersett to Hazard, at all the towns in the eastern part of Kentucky, all fords of rivers and hills from Lawrenceburg to the Cumberland Mountains. Had one horse stolen at Stanton, two killed under me while in battle, two shot so I had to leave them, had been bushwhacked on every road across the mountains.

I spent one month with 100 men at the Cumberland Gap and Goose Creek. Where the Laurel Gap and Williamsburg roads cross, one Dave Colston lived (now the town of Middlesboro stands there). I nursed Dave Colston when a boy and whiskey caused him to be an outlaw and murderer. Finally after he had been a member of congress, he killed his horse and shot himself to death. How times and scenes are passing through my mind, while I record these recollections of 60 years ago, how active I was then, how feeble I am now.

On the 20th day of August 1863 at Big Creek Gap Burnsides drove our pickets in and the 5th Tennessee became rear guard of all the troops of East Tennessee. I fought at each hill, each cross roads from Big Creek Gap to Hiwassee River. At Concord we had a heavy skirmish fight; at Lenoir's we had another; at the Junction of the Kingston and Lenoir Roads we had another. Here Col. Scott ordered me to take a Lieutenant and 100 men and contest ever foot of ground to the Loudon bridge. He soon rode back and said: "Adjutant, keep the enemy back till you hear my cannons fire from the south side of the river."

The Yankees pressed me back and the fight become hand to hand and no cannons fired. When I was pressed to the bridge, I had lost the lieutenant and 70 men. I fired the combustibles under the bridge and rode over under fire of two cannons. When I reached the south bank of Tennessee River a cannon shot killed one of my 30 men and his horse. Col. Scott galloped up and swore a bitter oath, said: "Adjutant, why did you fight so long." I answered: "Colonel, why did not your cannon fire." He swore, said some d--n man had spiked his cannons.

I rode out half a mile on the Philadelphia Pike. Col. Scott rode up and said: "Adjutant, did you destroy the ferry boat?" I said I had no instructions to destroy the boat. He ordered me back to destroy the boat. When I reached the river a man was pulling the boat to the north side of the river. I ordered him to bring the boat back. He pulled on. I ordered my boys to fire on him. He fell to the bottom of the boat. The two pieces of cannon opened fire on my squad.[15]

I moved through the main street of Loudon. Found Maj. Cobb and Captain Kuhn tussling over a dipper. I saw a bucket of whiskey sitting near them and each wanted the first drink. I dismounted and kicked the bucket over, their guns still firing on us. I saw a woman run across the street. A cannon ball ploughed the street near her, she fell.

Col. Scott kept me and my 29 men in the rear to Hiwassee River but we had little trouble keeping our pursuers off. When we crossed the river our regiment went on duty on Gen. Bragg's right. I posted pickets from Orchard Knob to the Tennessee River at the mouth of South Chickamauga Creek. Orchard Knob was covered with a thick scrubby undergrowth, as most of the line was to the river.

On the 6th of September we was ordered to Ringgold Gap on the Western and Atlantic Railroad below Graysville, Georgia. The creek ran close to White Oak Mountain. Much travel had made a pond of mud and water. Our regiment strung out in a long line. All of a sudden, Gen. Wilder shot a 4 front charge cutting the regiment in two. Col. McKenzie and 5 companies in front, Lt. Col. Montgomery and I with the balance of the regiment. Wilder charged us from the rear. Montgomery ordered me to about face Company I and charge in turn.

In driving them back one of their horses fell and blocked some 8 or 10 of them. I dismounted and clambered over rocks to make prisoners of them. A big Dutchman rose up, scraping the mud and water from his eyes and face and said: "Here I am, d--n take me." They drove our 4 companies up the side of the mountain. We did not get them stopped till we reached the top. Col. McKenzie stopped them at the gap of the mountain in the railroad line. Here I had my horse killed. William Runions was killed and several men had horses wounded.

Col. McKenzie went into camp and I had an ounce ball taken out of my right thigh. It had penetrated to the bone. I did not quit the line. We fought Wilder for the next 12 days from Ringgold Gap to Tunnel Hill. Wilder's Brigade had driven our regiment to Tunnel Hill. The next night Scott came to us with the balance of the brigade and we drove Wilder back to Peavine Creek. The 5t Tennessee Cavalry lost in these fights 17 men.

Morning of September 17th Col. Scott made Shelby Williams, his adjutant, write an order for me to take two men of the 5th Tennessee and charge the Yankee videttes off of Reeds's Bridge, proceed up the Bird's Mill Road and ascertain how many troops was on this road. I protested, but he was drunk. I took two of his regiment, as I did not expect to return and did not want to sacrifice my boys.

We charged the picket post. They fired, we kept up a fast gallop some 4 miles as they shot, but we escaped. At the Bird residence three men ran out and mounted and we ordered them under arrest. One of them, Woods Wilson, proved to be a Rhea County youth whom I knew. The other two was Michigan lieutenants. We crossed the railroad to the woods on the side of the mountain. The firing had scared some teamsters who drove fast, leaving a dense dust in their rear, which protected us. After allowing our horses to rest a while, we proceeded to camp with our prisoners. The drunken order had me on a wild goose chase for nothing.

On the evening of September 18th Col. Scott ordered the 5th Tennessee to charge and capture the Reed Bridge that spanned the creek on the Ringgold and Chattanooga dirt road. We took the bridge with a loss of one man. Nine o'clock that night we were ordered to report to Gen. Joe Wheeler's at Leet's Springs some 6 miles south. We had much trouble, the road was narrow and troops passing north. We reached there at 12 o'clock, sat on our horses two hours and were ordered back to the bridge. Wilder and Mitchell's brigade had charge of it.

Col. Scott ordered Lt. Hal Gillespie, who was in command of the Second Tennessee Cavalry (Col. H. M. Ashby was wounded) to charge and take the bridge. The Knoxville Company led the charge 1/4 of mile. They run into an ambush and Capt. Owens and some 10 or more men and horses were killed and many men and horses wounded. Confusion followed.

The road was through an old field covered with jack pine. The Fifth Tennessee was ordered forward. When I came to where the road was blocked with dead and wounded men and horses, I filed north. In passing through this dense scrub pine field, I came into the open 1/4 of a mile from where Wilder and Mitchell was lined up. I formed fours and charged their rear left flank, driving them south of the Ringgold Road. Col. Scott galloped up and ordered me to right face, dismount and every 4th man to take care of 4 horses (this was our first dismount) and the right of the regiment rest on the road. Scott's 1st Louisiana was on the left of the 5th Tennessee, the 2nd Tennessee on our right and Hart's 6th Georgia on the right of 2nd Tennessee.

The enemy had formed a battle line 1/4 mile from us and commenced to fire on us. We charged. They gave way and soon formed again. We charged each line they formed and we could hear Forrest and Pegram on our right. We knew the battle was on in earnest.

We had driven Wilder and Mitchell three and a half miles from the bridge past the Federal Hospital when they was reinforced by Baird's Brigade and the 8th Illinois Battery. There was a small field between our lines, some 200 yards across. This 8th Illinois Battery was raking our lines and making the boys lay low.

Col. McKenzie said: "Adjutant take A and D and capture that battery." Company D, my old company, had one commissioned officer. Company A had Capt. Jack Ragan and 3 lieutenants. I made the 6th commissioned officer when we started, as I was the last one of them to fall. We got the battery and every officer of the Bradley Company and the Hamilton Company had fallen and Orderly Sargent John D. Guinn was left in command of the remnant of these two gallant companies.

Capt. Ragan had two shots through his right arm. Lt. Sam Wilson, one shot through his left arm. Lt. Croxton, shot in the shoulder. Lt. Lansford[16], in the leg. I had a minnie ball through my left arm, a minnie ball through my left lung and two through my right leg below the knee. I had no bones broke, save two ribs near the breast bone. I was helped on my horse and the last thing I recollected was the top of a pine tree falling in front of me, cut off by a cannon ball.

The next I recollected I was in a provisional hospital on the banks of Chickamauga. I asked our regimental surgeon, S. H. Day, to pull a silk handkerchief through me. He said: "You will not live 5 hours." Brigade Surgeon Delaney said I could not live. I sent for the Division Surgeon. He was a conglomerate mixture of nationalities and I could not understand him. I only knew he was swearing. My wounds in the thigh had not healed and I determined I would not go to the Atlanta hospital with so many holes in my hide. I knew if I did, gangrene would get me. I ran away.

Sunday morning at sunrise found me at Ringgold, passing through the railroad gap at the stone church, some 3 miles south of Ringgold. I turned down Dogwood Valley. I had been forced to get off my horse so often and lay down and rest and my clothes was saturated with blood. I was bloody, muddy, and getting so weak from loss of blood I could hardly mount but by the help of John Loyd, who had run away from home and come to me.[17]

Near sundown Sunday evening, I came in front of a double hewed log house, two stories. I told John to help me down. I could go no farther. Soon a tall old gentleman, his wife and two daughters and probably a dozen small negroes came around where I was laying. The old motherly lady said to the girls: "Go fix the parlor bed." I said: "No. Give me the poorest bed you have got in a back room for I will not be able to move in the morning."

I was so weak I could not walk. The old gentleman and my faithful boy took me by the shoulders and arms and two negroes by my legs and carried me into a back room and laid me on a bed. Mr. J. C. Blackstock pulled my dirty, bloody clothes off of me and washed me and put some of his underwear on me. The good mother and her two daughters came soon with a cup of good coffee, bread and butter. This was the first bite I had eaten since Friday night. J.C. Blackstock, Esq., said: "What can I do for you now?" I said: "Get a bucket, a gallon and a half or two gallon, put a hole through the bottom so a drop of water will fall fast, and hang it over my breast and arm." Which he did.

There I lay for two weeks, the old mother and Miss Annie and Angeline giving me all the delicious and nourishing food they could find. I can't speak of their kindness without shedding a tear. They was as thoughtful as my wife, mother or sister could of been had they been with me.

John Loyd, my faithful beardless boy, would take care of our horses and go each day to a provisional depot nearby for any news he could gather. One day he came back, said Gen. Wheeler was going to raid Tennessee next morning. Soon he came in and said that Gen. Wheeler had started last evening. I said: "John, get our horses, I am going." The old Mother cried and said it would kill me.

At Mathis Shoal on Hiwassee River we overtook the command. The 5th Tennessee was in the rear. The word had gone from Chickamauga to my wife and relations that I had been killed. My father and brothers hunted for me but did not find any trace of me. When I overtook the boys, they gave the yell and it went from one end of the line to Gen. Wheeler's headquarters which was on the roadside hear Big Spring in Meigs County. He sent back to know what the howling meant. They told him I had come up and he sent for me to come to his quarters.

When I saluted the General he said: "You are the man I want to pilot me across the river at Cottonport." I said: "General, I have but one hand I can use and my wounds are all running." He then asked me whose brick house was on the north side of the river. I said: "Let me see the map that was lying on the ground at his side." I told him it was Capt. S.J.A. Frazier's. He said the Federal battery was there and asked where Capt. Latrobe's battery could find an elevated point to dislodge the Federal battery. I hold him. He ordered me to pilot Latrobe to the point.

Latrobe soon silenced the battery and Gen. Wheeler ordered me and a Mr. Delozier who lived in three miles of where I was raised to pilot the column across the river. The Federals had a log breastworks just below the mouth of Frazier's branch. When we reached the steam boat shoot [chute?], the Federals fired on us. Delozier and his horse was killed.

When we came to the Washington and Smiths X roads fork, I told Gen. Wheeler I was going to my father-in-law's two miles south of Washington. He said the 5th Tennessee was going to Dunlap, Sequatchie Valley by way of Smiths X road. I bid him adeau.

My faithful boy had led a horse for me, for my wife and baby boy to go south of the Tennessee River. When I reached my father-in-law's there was a scene long to be remembered. I got John Loyd to put my wife's saddle on the led horse and he joined the regiment, helped to capture Rosecrans' waggon train in Sequatchie Valley. Poor boy was wounded at Farmington and died and his grave is on the side of the pike from Columbia to Lewisburg.[18]

In two hours I got my wife with our baby boy was on our way to Cottonport. I had but one hand, my wife had our 18 months old boy in her left. The ford was a little up stream. I met a lieutenant of artillery at the river. I got him to tie the bridle bit of my wife's horse to mine so I could guide both.

We had to swim some twenty feet till we reached the shoal. The ford was rough and the water swift. When on the south side we went to Maj. Willam Russell's. Staid there on account of our boy being sick. Here my wife got the wad of my clothes off of the bones of my breast with a pair of button hole scissors.

Our William Gibbs boy died and I got permission of the Federals to bury him at our family burial ground. The Federal Post Commander permitted me, my wife, and Miss Sarah Russell to go under a flag of truce and our little Willie was buried under a flag of truce, the only one ever buried in Rhea County under a flag of truce.

I and my wife had some acquaintances at Ten Mile in the upper end of Meigs County and we went up there for a short visit. In returning to Mr. Ed Chattin's, where we got boarding, my wife's horse fell, crippled her and dislocated the mare's breast bone and she died. It commenced to rain and sleet. I took my wife to a house near the accident. Mr. Hutsell was a Union man and ordered me off of his porch. I told him my wife was hurt by a fall and was quite sick. He said no rebel could ever stay in his yard. I crossed the road to a board shed over a pair of blacksmith bellows. He ordered me into the road.

After some trouble I got my saddle off of my horse and my wife's saddle off of the crippled horse and wife on my horse, tied my saddle behind my wife and went to a Mr. John Stewart's who furnished my wife a horse to go to Mr. Chattin's. Here I staid till the fall of Mission Ridge November 27th.

A lieutenant of artillery was placed at Sullivan's Ferry with two pieces and he sent me word Mission Ridge had fallen and he was ordered to report to Gen. Bragg at Dalton. I left my wife at Mr. Ed Chattin's. It was a sad parting. She had lost two brothers and her only child and was among strangers and with no money.

At dusk November 28th I left her. Asa Johnson was with me. We rode to Bunker's Hill Ferry, could find nothing to cross the river in. I hollowed to the Sheriff of Meigs County. He was a Union man. He came to the water's edge. I told him who I was and that I wished to cross, that I was on my way to Dalton. He said he had a little vessel that would barely carry two. I asked if I could lead and swim my horse. He said he was afraid to undertake it. I told him to come and here I left my neighbor and friend, Asa Johnson, who had side pleurisy and could not walk. He went to prison and suffered prison life for 18 moths. Here I left my horse.

When on the south side of Hiwassee River the Sheriff told me there was Federal troops at Georgetown and directed me how to get around Georgetown. At day dawn I was on the south side of Georgetown and Cleveland. I lay in a wooded ridge in sight of the Cleveland road, saw many Yankees pass along the road.

When dark came I started for Dalton. I passed one mile south of Cleveland just below Jo Tucker's farm. When near the railroad track I ran into a Yankee picket post. I heard men walking on the railroad track. I found they were the videttes on duty. The others were all asleep. When they parted, I aimed to go out the way I came in but missed. I ran upon a large horse. I loosed him and led till I found a log and mounted and crossed the railroad between Cleveland and McDonald Station. Daylight came while I was in the neighborhood of Red Clay and I had to lay over all day.

I and horse was both hungry. At dark I got into the Cleveland and Dalton road and was arrested by our pickets and taken to General Bragg's quarters. He sent me to my regiment. They were on picket duty at Tunnel Hill.

I reached headquarters of the 5th Tennessee December 2nd 1863. The winter of 1863 and '64 was very severe. We had no tents. I was very thin and our food was poor rice crackers, clay peas boiled with a piece of beef. Col. McKenzie got me a place in the ordnance office where I could be in the dry.

The Army had been changed. Col. Scott was gone. Col. James T. Wheeler, Commander of the 1st Tennessee Cavalry, was in command of our brigade. I made my first report. Gen. Humes' ordnance officer said it was not right. I told him I had but one hand that I could use and asked him to correct the report. He was a smart aleck and cursed me. When he called me a liar I had hold of an old chair post. I gave it a swing and knocked the captain down. Col. Wheeler came into the room, arrested the captain and sent me to headquarters of the 5th Tennessee.

On the 27th of December President Davis relieved Gen. Bragg and placed Gen. J. E. Johnston in command of the army of Tennessee. There was much rejoicing among the men over the change.

In January 1864 our regiment was sent to Cave Spring, Georgia to recruit our horses. Gen. H. B. Davidson was put in command of our brigade. He was an old drunken West Pointer. One day he was drunk, driving around camps in a buggy. Told W. S. Redderick, of Company D, of the 5th, to untie his horse loose from the buggy and hitch his adjutant to the buggy. All three were drunk. When they started down a slant; the buggy pushed the adjutant to a trot. He fell and the buggy ran down grade. The shafts struck a bank and the General kept going till he struck the ground face foremost. Col. Montgomery preferred charges against him. I don't know what became of Gen. Davidson.

Gen. Johnston reorganized the Tennessee Army placing state troops together as much as he could. The 1st Tennessee Cavalry, Col. Jas. T. Wheeler; 2nd Tennessee Cavalry, Col. H. H. Ashby; the 5th Tennessee Cavalry, Col. G. W. McKenzie; and Lt. Col. Lewis' 9th Tennessee Battalion commanded by Maj. Akin composed Ashby's Brigade, Col. Ashby commanding.

I was sick. Col. Montgomery got a place for me to board. There fell a 4 or 5 inch snow. We moved back to Tunnell Hill and went on picket duty.

Gen. Johnston made an order on me through Gen. Wheeler directing me to go inside Gen. Sherman's lines and make a report as to his division and corps commanders and how soon Sherman would march. I and Lt. Col. Montgomery rode over to Gen. Wheeler's quarters. I asked Gen. Wheeler to relieve me from this trip. My wounds had not healed and I was in feeble health. Gen. Wheeler and I went to Gen. Johnston's quarters and Gen. Wheeler made the request. Gen. Johnston looked me in the face, and down to my feet and back to my face, said: "Adjutant Allen must make the trip." I saw in that grand old General a firmness of purpose but there was signs of sympathy that gave me the impression of goodness of heart. Gen. Johnston was the greatest and grandest general the war produced.

I went back to our quarters. Prepared 1/4 bushel of corn, some rice crackers and a piece of poor beef. Passed from the stone church on the east side of White Oak Mountain to a point I thought near Graysville, Georgia. On reaching the top of the mountain I found I was half mile northwest of Graysville. The sun near setting, I selected a place for my horse, poured out the corn, ate a piece of beef and rice crackers and waited for dark. I was covered by underbrush in sight of the railroad. Just at dark they posted their pickets. The pickets would walk some 1/2 mile, return, and come again. In the darkness I passed across the W. & A. rail road, waded Chickamauga, and struck the Graysville and Chattanooga dirt road.

I knew an old minister by the name of Julian. His home had been burned. He had an old maid girl named Julia and his other daughter was the wife of Lt. Sam Wilson. Lt. Wilson was one of the wounded officers when we took the 8th Illinois Battery. He had got back from the hospital. I called at the gate of the fence which was near the cabin door. The old gentleman came to the door, ordered me to leave at once. I called for Miss Julia. He again ordered me off. I said: "Is Mrs. Wilson in the room?" She came to the door. I said: "I have a letter for you from Sam." Miss Julia came to the gate. I told her I wanted her to put on her worst clothes and go abegging to each division and corps commander and learn the names of his commander on the right wing, left wing and his center, and I would be back about 10 o'clock next night.

I had posted pickets over this same ground and knew where a log school house had been torn down and each end of the logs rested on a log. These logs had been placed side by side and left a space some 30 inches from the ground to the logs. I went there, crawled under these logs, ate rice crackers, drunk water out of my canteen for 24 hours, the longest hours I ever spent in my life. After taps of the Federal Army I crawled out, stiff and sore. Went to Mr. Julian's. Miss Julia had succeeded in getting all the information I needed.

I started to go out the route I went in. They had moved their reserve picket post and I got so close they halted me. I ran. They fired and I went into the creek and waited till they quit searching for me. I got out, crossed the railroad and climbed the mountain, wet and cold. I was lost. When I got on top of the mountain after hunting a long time for my horse, he neighed. I mounted him in the dark, and wound about till day. I then struck for the old stone church, aiming to go to Mr. Blackstock's to get something to eat. When nearing the house she gave a sign to not come as the Yankee cavalry was between me and Tunnel Hill.

I then turned away to go to Trickum, a post office in the southern end of Dogwood Valley. Dark came on me. I was nearing the Trickum P.O. when I heard horsemen in my front. I about faced and soon heard horses in my front again. I dismounted, left my horse in the road. I clambered over rocks and logs on the side of Rocky Face Mountain, would sit down and rest and go again. When I reached the top, I turned north and soon was halted, told to give the countersign, hold up both hands and advance.

I said I could not hold up but one. When I advanced, the picket said: "You are a spy." I said: "What command do you belong to?" He said: "Coal's 54th Virginia." He took me to their reserve post. After many questions, they asked me if I was married. I told them yes. When and where? One of the boys said: "You say you married Miss Lizzie Thomison two miles below Washington?" I said: "Yes." He said: "She is my cousin." This was Wash Lewis of Roanoke, Virginia. He took me to Col. Coal's quarters. I told Col. Coal I had been in Sherman's lines on special duty and was anxious to get to Gen. Wheeler's quarters to make my report. He put me on his horse and sent me to Gen. Wheeler's quarters. It was about 3 o'clock A.M. I had not slept for 72 hours.

When we reached Gen. Wheeler's quarters, the guard said the General was asleep. The General heard me tell him that I must see Gen. Wheeler. He called out for me to come in. He got up off of his bearskin and said: "Adjutant, you look worn out. Lay down on my bed and I will wake you in two hours." When he woke me his breakfast (such as it was) was served. After the meal he said: "You can now make your report." I told him Gen. Hooker commanded the right camps, Gen. Baird, one division. That Gen. Thomas commanded the center and Gen. Jeff C. Davis, Sherman's left wing and that Sherman would advance in two weeks. Gen. Wheeler said: "This report will be very valuable to Gen. Johnston." He thanked me, mounted me and sent me to headquarters of the 5th Tennessee. On the 14th of February, 1864 I received the thanks of Gen. Wheeler, I here make a copy. Miss Lucy Wheeler asked me for the old blue paper but it will go to my children. I attach a copy to this paper.

Headquarters Cavalry Corps
Tunnel Hill, Ga. February 14th 1864

Lieutenant

I am directed by Maj. Genl. Wheeler to thank you in his name for the report of scout made by you and dated February 14th, 1864.

In as much as you have followed the instructions given you and state the authority for each report, the commanding general will be enabled to discriminate between facts and mere reports.

He directs me to say that this report is full and explicit and will prove valuable to the commanding general and plainly convinces [evinces?] exhibition of daring and intelligence in the officer by whom this scout was made.

Very respectfully, Lieutenant,
your obdt servant
W. E. Walls
A. A. A. Genl

To Lieut.
W. G. Allen
Co. D, 5th Tenn.
Cavalry Regiment
through
Col. James T. Wheeler
Commanding brigade

Fifteenth of April 1864 Gen. Wheeler through Col. McKenzie ordered me to report with 100 men to Pat Cleburne at the top of Rocky Face Mountain. At sunrise next morning when I reached the gap, I found a single man on the road. He had on a hunting shirt. I had never seen Gen. Cleburne. I asked him where I could find Gen. Cleburne's quarters. He said: "I am Gen. Cleburne. What orders have you?" I told him. He threw his hunting shirt back and I saw his stars.

Soon they rallied, and chased us up the side of the mountain, wounding two men and several horses. When I reached the top of the mountain, the General said: "You scattered them." They were getting close. The General said: "File right," and it seemed to me a thousand or more gun shots rang out and many of the Yankees were killed and wounded.

When I filed right I ran on top of my Rhea County boys who was on picket duty, J. T. Crawford[19] of the 26th Tennessee and N. P. Frazier of the 19th Tennessee Infantry.

That was the only time I ever saw the brave Pat Cleburne. He was brave as the bravest and he fell at Franklin, a noble --?-- upon the Franklin breastworks. He was a Jackson to the Tennessee Army. History should give him a good space.

On the 6th of April[20] we had a heavy skirmish. Sherman was feeling our strength. Picket fighting till the 4th day of May 1864 when Sherman's advance line shoved our pickets to the top of Tunnell Hill Ridge. On the 5th, we fell back to Crow Creek in front of Rocky Face Mountain. Sherman planted some 100 pieces of artillery along his front. On the 6th of May we fought the Crow Valley fight. Here we lost Lt. McGuffee[21] of Company B. He was an exceedingly good officer. He was the first man killed out of 601 effective men we had when the Johnston campaign commenced. On the 9th we charged and captured 173 wagons and most of the teams that was passing from Burnside at Knoxville to Sherman. Our cavalry lost 7 men, three of them from my old Company D.

On the 10th the 5th Tennessee and 8th Texas captured Gen. Grainger's whole brigade of horsemen when we got in his rear as he was pushing through Murry County, Georgia. When we charged we gave the Rebel yell. He hoisted the white flag. We did not lose a single man. The 11th of May we skirmished in front of breastworks on Cleveland and Dalton Road and Linon (?) roads and Catoosa Springs Road.

Gen. Martin let Sherman's troops drive him from Snake Creek Gap and across the Oostenaula River and Johnston was forced to evacuate his Dalton lines and take his Resaca lines. On the 12th our Division (Humes') occupied the Dalton ditches; the 13th we were forced to leave the Dalton trenches and were pressed so hard we fought a hard battle near Tilton, Georgia. Here, Lt. Col. Montgomery was so badly wounded he did not return till we reached Jonesboro, Georgia. Here I received my 7th gun shot wound in the right leg.

The 14th, the Battle of Resaca was fought and Gen. Humes' Division made a successful charge; driving Sherman's left across a rise. The 15th. Johnston left Resaca and fell back to Calhoun to keep Sherman from getting a straddle of the W. & A. railroad in his rear. The 5th Tennessee was in the rear as usual, and pulled a cannon over the pontoon to keep it from falling into the hands of Sherman. The 16th we had a heavy battle near Calhoun. Here I had a roan horse shot through the neck. We did not have ambulances enough to carry out our dead and wounded off of the field till a late hour in the night.

At this point Sherman had flanking columns to Rome, and to the Dahloniga Road at the foot of the mountains east of us. His line was 40 miles wide and Humes' Division was ordered from the right to the left to strengthen Kelly's Division of Martin's (Martin was superseded by Gen. Jackson). We was under fire day and night. After marching all night without forage or food and fighting Kilpatrick's and Garrard's or McCook's horsemen, they would attempt to turn our right or left. At Cassander (?) we lost several good men in battle on the Dahloniga Road. Humes' Division whipped Garrard and Kilpatrick's brigades in open field engagement. Then next day met and drove McCook to shelter.

On the 17th we fought a hard fight at Adairsville. Gen. Humes had hutted(?) in front of Cassville and our line along Tow String Creek was pressed hard. Gen. Kelley had his line so pressed the Ashby brigade had to reenforce him. Near Springville our brigade met Garrard's Brigade and drove them back. Their object was to take the W. & A. railroad south of Cartersville.

Gen. Johnston had issued orders that the retreat had been far enough, that we should give battle. Gens. Polk and Hood claimed the time was not well taken, that their lines was subject to cross firing. When these preliminaries were going on between the generals, Sherman's lines was pressing our cavalry so close that the two lines were close together. On Johnston's moving through Cartersville our horsemen had hard fighting to keep Sherman's advance off of the rear of our marching line. Sherman crowded Johnston hard as he crossed the Etowah River. By cavalry Wheeler's Corps was fighting on all roads leading to Alatoona.

When Humes' Division was nearing the river, Gen. Cox's Division of Infantry made a charge on Gen. Humes' Division of Cavalry. Humes' Division counter charged. In this hand to hand fight we lost heavily. We saved Johnston from having to form and fight when he was crossing the Etowah River. The night of the 20th we crossed the river under fire, burned the bridge. The 21st was spent in picket firing across the river at various points. On the 22nd late in evening, Gens. Garrard's and McCook's horsemen made an effort to cross the river at Mill Bridge, where the Cassville, Kingston and Cartersville road crosses the Etowah. Late in the evening Gen. Humes fell back on the Alatoona road because Gens. Stoneman and McLaw had crossed the river east of Etowah at Raccoon Ford.

After dark, on the night of the 23rd, Gen. Wheeler took charge of Humes' Division and moved east in the rear of McLaw's Brigade, captured his picket post, which was 7 of Col. R. K. Bird's regiment of East Tennessee Federal troops.

In the morning we were east of Cassville. We turned west and swept down on Sherman's supply train, capturing 173 wagons, loaded with army supplies. The teamsters fled, leaving some 100 waggons with teams attached. The morning of the 24th we passed into Johnston's line with our booty. Col. McKenzie was sick. Lt. Col. Montgomery wounded. We had no major and my duty was to obey others. Little food for man or beast, rain pouring night and day. Fighting night and day. Covering all roads leading to Marietta. Kelly's Division guarding Johnston's right and Gen. Jackson his left, Humes in the center and called for often. Ashby's Brigade and Allen's Alabama Brigade fought and held their grounds on Pack Mill and Powder Springs road against two corps of Sherman's army trying to get to Powder Spring in rear of Johnston.

While engaged in the New Hope Battle we held the line at a fearful loss. The 5th Tennessee lost 143 men, killed and wounded in three hours. Our regiment lost more men than at Chickamauga.

On July 14th, Col. McKenzie reported for duty. I sure was glad to see him. He had an order read from Gen. Wheeler promoting me to major[22]. I told him I would not leave my boys who I had called so often.

Our fighting continued in rain, on each road, at many churches and small creeks that are located in the Kennesaw Mountains till Sherman made his final attack on the Kennesaw line in front of Marietta. After his failure and when he outflanked Johnston and Johnston crossed the

Chattahoochee River, our cavalry occupied the Kennesaw did not get even an old waggon there as a trophy.

It was fight day and night to save the Boswell Bridge till Wheeler could get his cannons and waggons over the bridge. Here Humes' Division engaged Garrard's and Kilpatrick's horsemen in a hand to hand fight but Humes held the bridge till all was over and burned it behind him.

When Gen. Corse's Division crossed the river, Sherman's vandalism commenced in earnest. Women and children were driven out of their homes (125) and forced to go north of the river. I don't know where, but I saw soldiers following and burning each house as the inmates were forced to leave.

Humes' Division was sent west of Atlanta to meet a raid that had crossed the Chattahoochee river at Sand Town, some 40 miles below the Roswell Factory. We met, whipped, captured most of them. We drove them under the protection of Sherman's guns at Nickajack on the north side of the river. Then back to Roswell, fighting Cox's Infantry till the cavalry appeared on the Decatur road. Then it was day and night on all roads.

On the evening of July 17 Gen. Johnston issued orders to all of his command that the long expected battle would commence. Our army was in a good humor but here came orders that Johnston was displaced and Hood was put in command of the Army of Tennessee. Men with stout hearts wept.

Hood waited two days, gave Sherman time to unite his forces, then the slaughter commenced. July 22nd he lost 10,000 of that noble army and was forced to abandon Atlanta. Here again I sat on the hills west of Atlanta and saw the torch applied to all of the public buildings and many good homes. Then came Hood's orders to attack Sherman in open fields west of Atlanta. Here our brave officers and men were slaughtered by the hundreds and thousands.

While this was going on, Gen. Wheeler's small corps was split in twain, one half after Kilpatrick and his 6,500 horsemen, the other half after McCook and his 6,500, both to meet at Jonesboro and straddle the Atlanta and Macon railroad. Wheeler captured nearly all of Kilpatrick's gang near Jonesboro. Our brigade had been divided. Humes and two regiments was with Wheeler. Col. McKenzie had been left to watch Sand Town and the west of Atlanta.

McCook crossed the river at Sand Town and a race commenced between our brigade and McCook's 65 hundred for Jonesboro. We were on the inside road and beat McCook's first brigade and whipped them. At the same time Gen. Wheeler was in pursuit of Kilpatrick's remnant, drove them west of the railroad and soon they overtook McCook's 6,500 and about faced and commenced battle. Some 7 miles west of Newman they drove Wheeler with Humes' two regiments and Gen. Ferguson's Mississippians into the bend of Chattahoochee River.

Wheeler and half of his escort got away with the 9th Tennessee Cavalry who would not surrender. McKenzie with the 5th and 2nd Tennessee and 8th and 11th Texas hurried to the 9th Tennessee and charged through scrub pine and the captains were recaptured with 12 pieces artillery and 4,200 prisoners. McCook was drunk and we had recaptured Gen. Humes and Gen. Ferguson and their men and had more prisoners than there was of all Gen. Wheeler's forces.

Then back to Hood fighting on Lickskillet road till Hood had lost more than half of that gallant army. Then the president saw what a mistake he had made in relieving Johnston and placing Hood over the bravest and best army ever marshalled on any field in the world. On the 6th of August, Humes' Division fought their last fight on the railroad below Jonesboro.

In 33 days Humes' Division had fought 23 hard battles, skirmished every day, most of the time fighting Sherman's infantry at great odds. We had traveled over 300 miles in and around Atlanta, twice from right to left. The 5th Tennessee had fought every day and night from the 6th of April till the 6th of August. Had covered 133 miles of railroad. We had been on the railroad 104 days, had lost 304 men killed and wounded, over half of the 601 men we left Tunnel Hill with, April 6th 1864.

Gen. Wheeler moved to a point on Ocmulgee River above Macon where we shod our horses till 10th August. The 10th of August 1864 Gen. Wheeler marched till he struck the old Federal Road, made by Gen. Jackson when he was fighting the Indians, from Knoxville to Augusta along the front of the Georgia and Carolina Mountains. At Carter's Station Gen. Wheeler ordered me to take Lt. J. M. McKenzie of Company I and Lt. Langsford of Company A and 100 men and cut the wire between Tilton and Dalton, and burn the supplies at Dalton.

After tearing up the railroad track, I drove the pickets into Dalton with no trouble. When fired on they retreated. It was near day when we burned the depot. Gen. Wheeler had overlooked two pieces of cannon the enemy had on a rise nearby. When we fired the building, the blaze shot up. When the canister shot struck the roof it made a rocket. It gave us all a scare. We loaded ourselves with ham, good coffee and crackers. Moved out a mile on the Cleveland Road and had a good breakfast.

Just after our good meal our vidette fired and we soon formed for a scrap and it came. Col. McGavin who had a negro brigade advancing through a piece of new cleared land with his negroes, came through hog weeds as high as three heads. Here my 75 boys held this negro brigade for a while. They would flank us on either side. The fight lasted probably 30 minutes. I saw we could not hold them, we fell back and mounted, leaving Will Detherage[23] of Company B and Berry Talley[24] of Company D dead. Lt. Langsford[25] was never seen after that engagement. I think he was killed. Joseph McCrary lost a big toe.

Gen. Wheeler gave me orders to hold the Dalton and Cleveland road till he crossed the Hiwassee River at Cleveland [sic]. I captured 15 pickets, payrolled [paroled] them, passed to the right of town, back to the railroad at Charleston on the river, captured their pickets and had a little skirmish. Sent Lt. McKenzie up the river to find a crossing and crossed the river in the night. Near 12 o'clock I reached Riceville. Here I found a courier from Col. McKenzie at Athens, directing me to let all of Companies A, C, and I[26] go home and spend one night and meet next morning at Jo McKinkel's [McCorkle's] Mill on Good [Goodfield] Creek.

I and Lt. McKenzie parted at Shilo Church, he going home and I to Frazier's Ferry hoping I might get some word from home. When I got near Mr. George Gross's house, which was on the ferry road, I rode to the back of his orchard, tied my horse and went to his kitchen back door. Mrs. Gross met me and said: "Be careful, the Yankees have been busy all day up and down the road." She gave me a piece of bread and I went through the orchard, got some apples, cut my horse some stalks of corn, sat, watched the Yankees pass up and down the road till dark came. I had seen enough to satisfy me that I could not travel the road so I wended my way some 6 miles over logs and fences on the back of the farms.

Near sunrise I got to McKunkel's [McCorkle's] Mill, Only found John Atchley and Tom Whitesides who said the Colonel had sent them to tell me that the Yankees had captured some of his men and taken them to Hunter's Bluff on the Tennessee River where a camp of over three hundred was encamped and Capt. W. W. Lillard and the Colonel had gone in pursuit with all the men they could get and for me to meet them at the bluff.

Atchley and I and Whitesides moved out in a gallop over logs and fences, crossing the Locke Ferry road to Decatur near Lenoir [Leneas] Locke's residence. When in half mile of Hunter's Bluff we heard the battle open. A little nearer some 20 or 30 horsemen came dashing in full speed, shooting as they came. They were so panic stricken that they seemed wild. One of their shots killed my horse and I had to dodge from side to side to keep them from trampling me down. When they passed I found I was almost alone, Atchley and Whitesides gone, my horse dead.

The Colonel and his men had released 16 prisoners from a log corncrib, had killed and drowned nearly every negro in camp. The Colonel met Gen. Wheeler at Sweetwater and made the following report to Gen. Wheeler: "Found the enemy. Killed and dispersed them."

I was alone in this camp with dead negroes and horses, hungry and worn out. I could not overtake our cavalry, was in the enemy's land. I studied a few minutes, resolved to get north of river and probably would find a horse at my home town. I staid in the woods till dark. I went to the river, but could not get over. Found two dead negroes. After wandering around till giving out, I stopped at a straw stack, lay down and soon fell asleep. I was exhausted and feeble from want of food.

Next morning I saw Mr. T. J. Locke going towards the river. I whisteled, he looked and went back home. Soon his brother Lenoir [Leneas] came in sight. I whisteled and he about faced and went back. After a bit I saw a lady coming from the river. I again whisteled and she stopped and asked me what I was doing. Then I told her and said: "Jane Locke, I am almost starved." She was one of my neighbors in old Washington. She said: "Wait a little while. I will send you something to eat." She said: "I crossed the river in a hog trough, it is hid 200 yards below the ferry." Soon her uncle Lenoir [Leneas] Locke came along a path. He set a bucket down and went back. I found a good meal of bread and meat. My last meal was at Dalton just three days before.

Here I must digress to say that Lieut. J. H. McKenzie[27] was captured soon after he and I parted near Shilo Church and he went to prison and suffered all the horrors of prison life till after the close of the war. He is 91 years of age and is the only living Mexican soldier now alive in East Tennessee. He lives at his son's in Meigs County, Tennessee, Big Springs, P.O.

After working hard I got to the north side of the river. Went to Washington, scared every body badly and was three hours late or I would of met a scout Gen. Wheeler had sent from White's Creek. I searched the town, did not find a horse that could carry me up and down the mountain. I found one that I rode on. I could ride it on level ground. Went in less than a mile of my mother-in-law's home but dared not go. I rode to the foot of Walden's Ridge, led up. Rode over the top, led down to Phillip Hutchinson's. Told Mrs. Hutchinson to send the old mare to Mrs. Ruth Frazier's at Washington, and asked for food. The good old lady said there was not a bite in the house. I crossed a fence into the orchard, filled my pockets with apples and went to a fence corner near the main road leading down to Pikeville in Bledsoe County.

It was not long till I heard horses' feet on the pike. I peeped through the crack of the fence and saw it was a Confederate. I got on the fence and the boy said: "Adjutant, what are you doing here?" I told him, he dismounted and we proceeded down the road. At Aaron Swafford's we met four more of the 9th Tennessee. They took turns walking and letting me ride.

When we got to Pikeville, Maj. Akin had gone down the valley 8 miles to People's College. It was midnight when we reached Akin's camp. I told the Major I was starved and worn out. I had had but one meal from Dalton to here. He said: "Look in that camp kettle, you will fine something to eat." I told him I had my horse killed and I was afoot. He said: "Lay down here beside me and I will mount you in the morning." In the morning he mounted me on a small roan horse and a farmer's saddle.

At Altamont we found Col. Paul Anderson's 4th Cavalry. He was preparing to charge Col. Bill Stokes' regiment who were in a stockade. We made the charge but failed to get in. It so happened in that charge that Lieut. Delaney and I struck the stockade at the corner of a store house. Delaney was feeling for a match to set the house on fire. Someone inside mounted something and killed Delaney, and one man struck at me with a saber and split my horse's ear. I galloped away under the protection of the house, captured a negro in full federal outfit, turned him over to Col. Anderson. Anderson talked through his nose, called his adjutant and told him to courtmartial the negro.

Anderson lost 7 men in this charge. We went from Altamont to Winchester, captured a waggon train of supplies on the side of the mountain, destroyed the supplies at Winchester. At Decherd it was raining and the dark night was on us. Our column stopped. Dr. Delaney[28] and I was riding by the side of each other. We got nervous and rode forward to learn what was the trouble. We found the men was asleep. We rode forward, rode to a vidette post, asked where Col. Anderson's headquarters was. We was answered with a volley from the pickets. We retraced our steps to find our command gone.

We took the other fork of the road and soon found the railroad track. A train was coming slowly towards Murfreesboro. The Doctor and I filled the stock gap with ties and waited results. They moved so slowly and stopped and the road and woods was soon lined with soldiers. I went into the river and kept under water till the hunt was over. The train passed. The brush was thick and I soon lay down and went to sleep. I never heard what become of Dr. Delaney.

When I awoke I was in a cedar thicket. I had lost my horse. I listened for sounds. I heard horses' feet on the pike. I moved up close so I could see who was passing. I made myself known. I found it was Gen. Williams' Kentucky Brigade. I asked to be sent to his quarters. I found him drunk, as usual. He mounted me and told me to stay at his quarters. Soon Gen. Dibrell came. He and Williams agreed to charge and take Murfreesboro. We made two unsuccessful charges. Soon came Gen. Felix Robertson with his small brigade. He was the ranking officer. He ordered a third charge. We failed. We could hear Gen. Wheeler's guns at Lavergne. We moved down to Cornersville. Here Robertson and Williams disagreed, Robertson followed Gen. Wheeler[29].

Gen. Dibrell had many men who had gone by their homes in Middle Tennessee. Williams pressed me as his guide and started for East Tennessee, Dibrell along gathering his men. Williams was drunk and I protested against being the guide for I did not know the country.

At Harriman, Williams stopped to feed and rest, someone stole his pants. He was a whiskey bloat and had to stay in his room till he could get a pair of pants made that would go around his bloated corpulency. He had two of the 2nd Tennessee Cavalry, who happened to be along, arrested and hung. We went from Harriman to Rogersville in Hawkins County. Here I ran away from him and went to Gen. J. C. Vaughn who was camped at Limestone, 6 miles below Jonesboro.

I told Gen. Vaughn that I had run away from Williams and if Williams made requisition for me that I did not want to be turned over to him. I had three brothers in Vaughn's old 3rd Tennessee: T. A., Maj. George W., and V. C. Allen[30]. Vaughn said: "Go visit your brothers and the Rhea County boys. I will take care of you." Brother George was gone to Richmond for funds to pay off Vaughn's Division.

When the Federals raided the Virginia salt works, Vaughn's Division was on their way to meet the raiders. Near Jonesboro we met Brother George. Gen. Vaughn said: "George, I am glad you are back. I need you." George patted a large pair of leather saddle bags and said: "General, what shall I do with this?" The General said: "Turn it over to Adjt. Allen." I knew the bags was full of Confederate money. I said: "No." Gen. Vaughn turned to his adjutant and said: "Make an order on Adjt. Allen to take charge of the saddle bags." Adjt. Dave Blevins made the order. Gen. Vaughn said: "Ride with us till I tell you when to leave us." Near Abingdon, Virginia he said: "Go south till you cross the South Fork of Holston River and stay till day after tomorrow and came back in time to fall in with us as we return from Saltville."

Here again I had trouble to get anything to eat for myself or my horse. The Prestons and such old men as they said: "No, we won't feed a man that is running away from a fight." I would not tell them why I was alone. I had to press my food for myself and horse. Slept in a horse stall with Confederate money for a pillow.

When I reached the pike, Vaughn's command had passed some three hours earlier. I rode to Bristol. I knew John King. He was owner of the Salt Works. I went to his house, stayed all night. Brother George's wife was there. She was Mr. King's niece. She talked loud and when I got to bed it was late. Mr. King had a yellow girl to help in the house and she had a yellow beau.

I got a late start. Dark overtook me near Tom Nelson's home above Jonesboro. I passed into a dense woods, whistling. All at once, a cap burst near me by the side of the road. I threw myself to the right. As I moved over I drew my pistol. The robber, bushwhacker, fired and glanced my side, the ball made a blood blister on my left thumb. I fired twice and put spurs to my horse. I soon heard horses' feet in my rear. I thought I was pursued. I afterward learned it was Maj. Tom McConell (later Chancellor). He had heard the firing and thought the bushwhacker was after him and I thought his horse's feet was a bushwhacker after me.

Next morning a negro sent in to Vaughn's quarters for a surgeon to come and take a ball out of his heel. I told Gen. Vaughn I would go out and kill him. Vaughn assented but soon said: "No. If you do that it will probably cause some women and children's home to be burned." This same negro had waylaid Maj. McLin and killed him. McLin was captain of the Jonesboro company which was Compny H in the 5th Tennessee Cavalry.

Gen. Williams came and made requisition on Vaughn. Instead of turning me over to him, Gen. Vaughn gave me transportation by way of Danville, Virginia, Greensboro and Raleigh, North Carolina, and Columbia, South Carolina, and Augusta, Georgia to Gadsden, Alabama. Gen. Wheeler, while I was away, had made a trip to lower East Tennessee, Cleveland, and assaulted and captured the block house at Dalton and passed into North Alabama. I had left my horse in East Tennessee, and I walked from Gadsden to Collinsville where the 5th was on duty. W. O. Jones of Company C gave me a fine mare.

When Gen. Corse pressed us out of North Alabama, the bridges were burned and we had to swim the Coosa River. In swimming, our horses would drift below the ford and the banks were so steep our horses could not get out. Gen. Wheeler ordered me to make a detail of good swimmers to mount and swim the river with 4 or 5 horses tied to the tail of the one rider and then to one after another. I detailed Luke King and he rode and swam 38 horses and swum back[31]. When he had carried the last trip a Georgia Colonel told him if he would swim his mule over he would give him a $100 bill. Luke King swam the Coosa River on that chilly November day on horseback 39 times and back 39 times without a horse. He now lives at Washington, Rhea County, 89 years old, a very poor man but a very good citizen and was paroled at Charlotte, North Carolina, April 27th, 1865.

Hood was in Tennessee, Sherman's cavalry was raiding and destroying everything they could find. Near Macon they met some of Gen. Jackson's command and he whipped them. On their wild run to get away, Wheeler, with Humes' Division, struck them and the panic among them was great. In crossing a deep washout some of their horses and men fell. They stampeded over them till the ditch was full of men and horses trampled by the flying, scared crowd till you could see the bones of men with the flesh torn off by horses' hooves.

On Buck Horn [Head] Creek we encountered the Kilpatrick and Garrard brigades and whipped and captured 300 or more. Here I got a large bay horse. (Here Gen. Wheeler took a boy, J. M. Todd, up behind him and crossed the creek. The boy had had his horse killed. J. M. Todd belonged to Company I, 5th Tennessee).

Gen. Wheeler ordered me to take the prisoners to Augusta. While waiting for a train out of Augusta, I had the prisoners in a field. Soon most of them was asleep. One came to the guard near where I was and talked to the guard. An old Georgian came along. He had a big stick. All of a sudden he knocked the Yankee over. The Yankee was sitting down. I hollowed to Armstrong to knock the Georgian down, which he did.

When I came back, Col. McKenzie told me Gen. Wheeler wanted me at his head quarters. I went and Gen. Wheeler said: "An old farmer has come and made charges against you for having a soldier to knock him down." I said that I saw him in the yard. Gen. Wheeler called the farmer in and told him to state why I ordered him knocked down. I said: "That old man knocked a prisoner down without warning and I told the guard to knock him." The General said to the old man: "If you want to fight, go join a company and fight but don't dare to hit a prisoner." Turned to me, and said: "Adjutant, you can go back to your regiment."

Another raiding party started to Augusta. We were in that lonely pinery when Gen. Dibrell came in command. We had a hard battle. We lost 7 men killed, amongst them Lt. Col. Shaw of the 18th Battalion[32], one of Gen. Dibrell's most trusted friends. We dug a ditch, wrapped their old blankets around them, laid them in the ditch. Gen. Dibrell stood with uncovered head, with tears streaming down his cheeks, gave orders to fire the salute. There we left those gallant boys in the lonely pine land and nothing but the singing wind, song of the wind.

On the 30th of December 1864 we crossed the Savannah River on a steam boat and went to a point 15 miles east of Savannah. Here I made my first report of our regiment after we left Tunnel Hill. Hood had squandered the grandest army ever assembled. Squads of them were passing to their old beloved Joe E. Johnston. When Gen. Lee asked him to take charge and reorganized the remnant, his noble big heart could not say no.

When Charleston fell, we moved up the Savannah River near Augusta. Gen. Wheeler ordered me to take Companies A, B, and I (these three companies had 123 men rank and file) and report to Gen. McLaws at Branchville, South Carolina. When I reported, Gen. McLaws sent me 7 miles up the Orange River to take and hold the bridge till his waggon train and men passed on their way to Columbia and when he passed he would send a courier.

Company A, Capt. Jack Ragan, drove the Yankees away; Capt. W. W. Lillard and Capt. Jno. Blythe could not agree. Capt. Lillard wanted to take command and here the Captain gave me much trouble. Gen. McLaws did not send a courier and I was cut off from our troops for three weeks and had trouble on the Seven Notch road with the tide on one side and Gen. Wilson with 1,000 horsemen after me. Three times he forced us into a fight. We had just men enough to make a bold charge and they were always ready.

At Darlington we captured 40 negroes who had robbed the women and old men of all the jewelry they could get. I lined them up, got the jewelry and gave them 39 lashes each. We went from Darlington to Florence. Gen. Roberson was in command. All the heavy guns from Charleston had been moved to Florence. Gen. Roberson had a brigade of old men to command these guns. Wilson's 1,000 men were sent here to capture the war materials. Gen. Roberson had agreed to set me and my men across the river.

On the morning Wilson attempted to capture Florence, the pickets commenced firing on all the roads that come into Florence. Capt. Lillard was nervous. I consulted with Capt. Blythe and Capt. Ragan. We agreed to cut our way out rather than be captured. Ragan's company to follow me and then Blythe and then Lillard. We did not let Lillard know what we intended to do. When the Yankees drove the poorly equipped old men in sight on the Darlington road, we charged and they fell back across the railroad and lined up.

At the railroad crossing of a dirt road there was a grade made by cutting the dirt road down to a level, making the dirt road narrow. As we entered this cut, one J. C. Smith, of Company A, forged beside of me (he always was on a small mule, being very tall, he did not look like a soldier). As we entered this cut the Yankees poured a volley into our advance. One shot my horse in the breast, entering his heart. He sank down and one shot hit Smith's mule in the head. He fell and the two horses filled the narrow road. Jack Ragan dismounted, came up and he and I pulled as the horse struggled till one man in single file could pass.

While we was lining up, the Yankees kept firing on us. When the last man came through it was Capt. Graham of Co. G, who had been under arrest since the Resaca Battle, May 14 and been in my way many times. I dismounted him and took his horse (I should of stated that while we were in camps above Savannah a pine tree fell on the fine mare W. O. Jones had given me and killed her).

After we had whipped them and returned to Florence, I was again afoot. Gen. Roberson gave me a note of thanks for saving his post and gave me a black horse I rode home. This was my 19th horse. I had lost five killed in battle, 6 wounded and left, 1 stolen at Stanton, Kentucky, 3 abandoned to keep from being captured, 1 left in East Tennessee, 1 fell and killed herself while my wife was riding her and 1 the tree fell on.

Gen. Roberson set us over the Peedee River where we encountered a brigade of Sherman's Cavalry and formed to charge them at Martin, South Carolina. While waiting their moves, they turned two pieces of artillery loose at us. One shot hit our flag and tore it to shreds, leaving the lower end of the staff in the hands of the bearer. The good women of Martin made us a new one that night for keeping the Yankees away from their homes.

We joined Col. McKenzie in time for the Fayetteville fight where we came so near getting Gen. Kilpatrick. We got his woman, his clothes, and the finest pair of boots I ever saw and some old planter's baroche he had taken to haul his woman around in and a good supply of rations.

On 19th of March we fought our last battle at Bentonville, North Carolina. Here our Lieutenant Colonel and 4 men was wounded and parolled in the hospital. The once gallant, proud volunteer regiment of 1308 now had 244. 31 of these gallant boys lie mouldring in northern prison graves. Some of them I never knew what became of them. Today I can only find but one of my old Bradley County Company D, B. F. Loyd of Pikeville, Bledsoe County.

I hope and pray these scrambled pages may enable you to get some facts that will help to give our southland the honor that is due them, especially the old Volunteer State of Tennessee.

John Trotwood Moore, State Historian. If I can help you in any way, call on me. I am 86 years old and don't use glasses, I have a good recollection. Yours truly

Dayton, Tenn.
Jan'y 10th 1922, W. G. Allen

38. *When and where discharged:*
At Charlotte, North Carolina, on twenty day of April 1865.

39. *Describe your trip home:*
May 4th 1865 we mustered, passed through Ashville, N.C. At gap of mountain we found one Col. Kirk and some 3 or 4 hundred bushwhackers. Robert Kirk commanded our horses and side arms

of the officers. After a long parley between Col. McKenzie and Kirk, Col. McKenzie ordered me to bring forward the officers. Kirk's men had heaped insult on our boys by riding along the line cursing the G.D. rebels, pulling their hats and old caps over their eyes till the men was ready for any kind of a fight.

We had 14 officers (out of 44) and 244 men out of the original roll of 1308. I lined these 14 officers up in front of Kirk's regiment, told Col. Kirk to open ranks and let us pass, if he did not somebody was going to get killed. When I ordered the men to cock their pistols, Kirk opened the way and we passed down the Watauga into Tennessee.

When we came to Maryville in Blount County, Col. McKenzie ordered me to take one man and go ahead to Sweet Water and arrange for rations and horse feed for all who had not left for their homes. When I and J. M. Thompson got to Sweetwater, the Commander of the Post took my side arms and our horses, placing us under arrest. The Post Commander would not pay any attention to our paroles. I demanded to be sent to Knoxville and when I reached Knoxville the Post Commander ordered me back to Sweetwater, giving the Post Commander at Sweet Water instructions to give me my saber, pistol, and our horses. Col. McKenzie and men came and could not find me. They passed down Sweet Water Valley.

I and Thompson mounted and rode to Thomas Prigmore's, four miles west of Sweetwater. (I was well acquainted with the old man and his wife. The Federals had taken him to his barn and tied a rope around his neck to make him tell where his money was hidden for he was reputed to be rich. His wife followed with a large butcher knife in her hand. When the Yankees pulled him off of his feet, the wife told them they could kill her but that she was going to cut the rope. Which she did, and they did not kill her. Old Mr. Prigmore lay on the barn floor till he recovered strength enough to walk back to the house). When we rode up to the gate she motioned us to the barn. After a time Mrs. Prigmore sent us some cornbread and a small piece of meat. Prigmore was one of the richest men in Sweet Water Valley.

Early next morning we mounted and rode to Smith's Ferry on the Tennessee River. Could not get across the Tennessee River. We then went down the River to T. J. Locke's Ferry where we got something to eat and fed our horses. At night we crossed the river and I arrived at home of my father-in-law two miles below Washington, Rhea County, Tennessee.

I found my good wife and a little dog that I had left. My home and fences were burned and my two children lay in the Frazier cemetery. I moved into a double log stable and went to housekeeping on a sifter of meal and a small piece of bacon (borrowed). I planted about 6 acres of corn. Dr. John Hoyal was my friend and had furnished me a little corn for seed to feed my horse on and make me and my wife bread. (I should have stated I got home May the 10th, 1865.)

I was given a note to leave the county in 10 days or his legion of 103 would hang me to a limb of a tree that stood in front of my cabin, signed by J. C. Wilson, Captain. I knew Wilson well before I went into service. At the end of 10 days Wilson rode up to the door and said: "Here you are, you G. D. rebel. I will be back in two hours and hang you." I stepped in the cabin and drew the load that was in my 44 pistol; loading it carefully and then sat in my door, waiting for him to return, intending to kill him. Here I spent two of the longest and most miserable hours of my life.

They had called an old man, my neighbor John Howell, to his door and shot him down while his daughter Rachel held him by the arm. They had hung Jim Fraly, had killed Hollis Dunn at his home, Samuel Brady at his barn, and beat up old man J. D. Chattin and George Todd and others on the streets of Washington.

My poor wife sat in silence, while I waited for Wilson but he did not come. I was plowing my patch of corn when John D. Rains and a Mr. Wilhoit of Bradley County came with five others I did not know, told me to stop plowing, lay my plow gears off of the horse. I did not. Mr. Wilhoit layed the gears off and led the horse away. As he passed the door of my cabin, I told my wife to throw me my old jacket. She was crying and begging me to not follow them. I walked and run some four miles in their rear. When nearing Smith's X Roads John Rains told Wilhoit to drop the bridle reins of my horse and said: "That d--n fellow will follow us to Chattanooga." I said: "J. D. Rains, I know you. You deserted my old Company D, 5th Tennessee Cavalry.[33]"

My next trouble, J. P. Walker, U.S. Deputy Marshal, came and arrested me for treason and would not take a bond for my appearance at Knoxville for the September term of Federal Court. As he stepped in the door my wife drawed a chair to strike him. "You can't enter my house after treating my sister and sister-in-law as you have."

I offered him a $200.00 bond but he would not take it. At Athens, I appealed to John Stover, another deputy U.S. Marshall, and he took my bond. After much expense and much worry attending the Federal court at Knoxville, President Grant --?-- when President Davis was relieved out of Prison. I have not been tried for treason till this good day.

One Samuel Lowe of Hamilton County sued me, Col. J.W. Gillespie, Dr. John Hoyal, Maj. F.J. Paine and Esqr. Wm. Clack for $25,000 each. We went to the old Harrison Courthouse to set up a defense. Was met at the courthouse door by Governor Brownlow's band of thieves and robbers and told we could not enter the court house. Col. J.W. Gillespie and Judge D.M. Key was fast friends. Gillespie was Colonel of the 43rd Tennessee Infantry and Key was Lieutenant Colonel. Judge Key came to us and said: "You had better return to the steamboat without trying to set up any defense as this mob will kill some of you." We started back and they followed and took Dr. Hoyal's overcoat.

I could give other mobs in Rhea County. We had three, the Johnson Hoge Seven, the Fugate Seven, and the William Phar Seven, some Negroes. I and my brother-in-law was attacked in our own house by the Johnson mob, one negro in the bunch. Brownlow's militia and his judges and sheriff was a gang of robbers and some of them --?--
But I have said enough. W. G. Allen

40. *Describe your work after the war:*
I made a little crop in the fall of the year. Judge Locke's nephew, Hanibal Paine, was a merchant in Washington. He died and Judge F. Locke sold me his stock of merchandise on a credit and I made good. Was able to buy a good farm. Trusted a friend and lost all.

41. *A sketch of your life after the war:*
I farmed and traded in grain, horses, and cattle, and sold goods. Lived at Washington on a farm and have been a member of Southern Methodist Church since August 20th 1850.

42. *Details of your father:*
Valentine Allen. Born near Fateville, Bedford County in 1809, Tenn. Lived in Larkinville, Ala. two [years], 6 yrs in Miss. Came to Rhea County in 1843. He had little education. He served as peace officer in Scotts' war with the Florida Indians in 1834.

[He] belonged to Capt. Waterhouse's company of old men. Maj. Wilkers [Welcker's] Battalion was captured and placed in the Kingston jail, Roane County, then taken to Chattanooga. Staid in prison there two months and were taken to Nashville, put in the penitentiary for three months. From there to Louisville, Kentucky and was paroled out of Louisville penitentiary by Gen'l Palmer and placed north of the Ohio River with instructions not to go south and make his own living. He was sick and feeble. Robert Kyle and Perry Able was Rhea County old men and bound by the same terms as father. Perry Able died and his family has never been able to find his grave.

Father did not get home till June 1865. He was paroled out of the penitentiary by order of Gen'l Palmer. W.G. Allen was paroled by Gen. J.E. Johnston's terms with Gen. W.T. Sherman, April 24, 1865 at Charlotte, N.C. Brothers T.A. Allen, G.W. Allen, and V.C. Allen was paroled May 8th, 1865 by order of President Davis at Washington, Georgia.

My only sister, Barbara F. Allen was paroled by order of Gen. Steedman at the corner of Market and 7th Street, Chattanooga, March 9th 1865 (see page 154 of [*Confederate*] *Veteran*, April 11th 1911 for the arrest and treatment of the only organized company of women in the Confederate states[34]. They were arrested and marched to Chattanooga under guard of Capt. John P. Walker, U.S. Captain, by Lieutenant Col. Goins, U.S.A. I have the original order and correspondence between Col. Goins and Miss Captain Mary McDonald and names of 31 girls arrested and taken to Chattanooga from the best families of Rhea County.

When he was released, my father was in Indiana, aged and weak, had been in a little cabin that a copperhead man had furnished him to shelter him from the wintery blast of 1865. He wrote my mother that he wanted to come home, had no money and was not able to walk. I rode to Chattanooga and borrowed $20 from Wm. Crutchfield who was a Union man. I told him what I wanted it [for] and I did not know when I could pay him back. He gave me the money and I sent it to Father. He got home in June.

43. *Details of your mother:*
Ann Frazier. [*Daughter of*] Beriah Frazier and Barbara Gibbs, their home in Frazier's Bend on Tenn. River.

44. *Remarks on ancestry:*
My grandfather Valentine Allen came to South Carolina in 1774, married and settled in South Carolina. He was Scotch Irish. My grandmother was Scotch and French, came to South Carolina. Her maiden name was Barbara Collins. Grandfather fought for independence of America and was at the Battle of New Orleans under Gen. Carroll. Grandfather Frazier was under Gen'l Green in wars for America's independence.   Dayton, Tenn. Jany. 1922 W. G. Allen

45. *Names of members of your company:*

46. *Name and address of living veterans:*

WILLIAM F. BLEVINS

William F. Blevins was born October 27, 1835, in Rhea County (portion that became Meigs County the following year). After the war, he read law and obtained a license to practice, but abadoned the profession for mercantile pursuits. In 1870, he was appointed Clerk and Master of the Chancery Court of Meigs County, a position he held for 12 years. On May 11, 1871, he married Mary E. Russell. Early in 1883, William moved to Darwin Station (Evensville) in Rhea County, where he purchased a store house. He died in 1925 in Rhea County and was buried in Buttram Cemetery.

Blevins' questionnaire was neatly completed in ink.

The list of members of his company, given in response to Questioin 33, is correct except that Tim Howell is not listed on regimental rosters.

BLEVINS, W. F.; 2Lt (I) 5th (McKenzie's) Tennessee Cavalry Regiment

Residence:
Enlisted: July 19, 1862 at Shiloh [Church], Tenn by W. W. Lillard for 2 years
Age: 27 on March 11, 1864 roll
Paroled: May 3, 1865 at Charlotte, North Carolina

<u>Muster Rolls</u>
Present   1862 July 19 - Oct 31 (I - 2nd Bn)
Present   1862 Nov - Dec   (I - 5th Regt)
Present   1863 Feb 25   (I - 5th Regt)
Present   1863 Mar - Apr (I - 5th Regt)
--------   1864 Mar 11 at Tunnel Hill (Lillard's Co)
--------   1864 Nov - Dec   (I - 5th Regt)
        Present for duty

QUESTIONNAIRE A
January 3, 1922

1. *Name and Address:*
   W. F. Blevins, P.O. Dayton, Rhea County, Tenn.

2. *Current age:*
   86

3. *State and county of birth:*
   Meigs County, Tenn.

4. *State and county when enlisted:*
   Meigs County, Tenn.

5. *Occupation before the war:*
   Merchandising and farming.

6. *Occupation of your father:*
   Farmer.

7. *Value of property you owned:*
   No property, only my interest in store.

8. *Slaves owned, if any:*
   None.

9. *Land your parents owned:*
   About 1,300 acres.

10. *Value of parents' property at onset of war:*
    About two thousand dollars.

11. *Kind of house your parents owned:*
    A frame 4 room house with one story house, porch on each side.

12. *What kind of work you did as boy and young man:*
    As a rule, farm work.

13. *Kind of work your father and mother did:*
    Father worked on farm and in griss mill. My mother spun, wove cotton and flax, and made clothes for a family of nine and cooked for her family.

14. *Servants your parents kept, if any:*
    Servants at intervals.

15. *Was honest toil respected in your community:*
Perfectly honorable by all. Good citizens were treated alike.

16. *Did white men engage in toil:*
Yes, sir. Rich and poor alike. Plowed and hoed with their negroes.

17. *Did white men idle while others worked:*
Not over two percent of those days.

18. *Did slave owners mingle or feel themselves better:*
No distinction among men of character.

19. *At public gatherings did slave owners mingle freely:*
They certainly did, no distinction.

20. *Was there a friendly feeling between owners and non-owners:*
Their certainly was. Their was no animosity in any way.

21. *Did slave owners have a political advantage:*
No difference was shown in any contest. They all voted together as free men.

22. *Were opportunities good for a poor young man:*
Where a young man had character and industry he could save enough to buy a small farm.

23. *Did slave owners encourage or discourage poor young men:*
All were encouraged to make good citizens of the good classes of men.

24. *Kind of school you attended:*
Public schools in our neighborhood when small and two years at the Decatur Academy.

25. *How long did you go to school:*
Three years in all.

26. *How far was it to the nearest school:*
About 2-1/2 miles and one three miles. We walked.

27. *What schools operated in your neighborhood:*
The public schools and Decatur Academy.

28. *Was your community school private or public:*
Usually private. The Academy was kept. We paid for our subscription.

29. *How many months a year did it run:*
About three months.

30. *Did boys and girls attend regularly:*
Fairly good.

31. *Was the teacher a man or a woman:*
    First to a woman. The rest of my teachers was men.

32. *Year and month you enlisted:*
    July second at Shilo Church, Meigs County, Tenn.

33. *Your Regiment: Members of your company:*
    Company I, 5th Tenn. Cavalry, Col. G. W. McKenzie.
    Lt. W. F. Blevins   Harrison McMillen
    W. C. Godsey, Private   Hiram O. Beavers
    Jerry M. McKenzie, 1st Lt.   Pleas Hunter
    ------ Blevins, 3rd Lt.   John Blevins
    Tim Howell

34. *After enlistment where was your company sent:*
    To Chattanooga. Reported to Gen. Bragg and assined to Maj. Lewis' Battalion till after Perryville Battle in Kentucky. Was on Bragg's escort from Sparta.[35]

35. *How long before your first battle:*
    Fought battle of Munsfordville, Kentucky.

36. *Your first battle:*
    Munfordsville, then Perryville and after Perryville Company I went to 5th Tenn.

37. *Your experience in the war:*
    The Fifth Tennessee was Bragg's rear from Perryville to Sickamore Shoals in East Tenn. In many fights in Ky. and East Tenn along the Gaps in East Tenn. Was the rear guard from Big Creek Gap to Charleston on Hiwassee; posted pickets on Bragg's right from Orchard Knob to River; fought Gen. Wilder 12 days on the road from Ringgold to Tunnel Hill; in the Chickamauga Battle; and under fire 120 days from Dalton to Jonesboro, Ga.; battles of Resaca, Calhoun, Atlanta, Kenesaw, New Hope Church, all around Atlanta.

38. *When and where discharged:*
    At Charlotte, N.C. April 26, 1865. Left for home May 4, 1865.

39. *Describe your trip home:*
    After we [left] Ashville, one Col. Kirk who had 3 or 4 hundred bushwhackers lined up his men and demanded our horses. And the 14 officers had side arms, rode to the front and told Kirk somebody would be killed if they did not let us pass. They concluded to let us pass.

40. *Describe your work after the war:*
    I helped my Mother till I was appointed Clerk and Master. I held that office 12 years. Read law, obtained license but did not practice. Went into the Mercantile business.

41. *A sketch of your life after the war:*
    I was a merchant for a time in Meigs County. In February 1882 I moved to Evensville and sold goods till June 1892 I moved to Dayton.

42.   *Details of your father:*
  James Blevins. [Born] 1805 in Sullivan County, Tennessee. [Lived in] Meigs County and died at age of 48 years. He was a Justice of the Peace in Meigs Co.

43.   *Details of your Mother:*
  Ruth Rockholt. [Daughter of] Frank Rockholt and [his wife] I don't know her [name].

44.   *Remarks on ancestry:*
  I never knew any of my [ancestors]. Grandfather and father were English men and his wife Irish and my mother was Scotch descent.

W. F. Blevins
Dayton, Tenn. Jan'y 3rd, 1922

45.   *Name the members of your company:*

46.   *Name and address of living veterans:*

JOSEPH EDWARD CHARLTON

Born April 2, 1840, Joseph Charlton was 21 years old when he joined McLin's cavalry company in December 1861. He was present at every muster until transferring June 10, 1863 to Carter's scouts, sometimes referred to as Wheeler's Scouts. Records for that unit are incomplete: it was with Gen. Hood on his campaign to Nashville and appears to have dissolved afterwards, the men individually attaching themselves to other units until the war ended a few months later. Some of the men made their way to Johnston's army in the Carolinas; others, such as Charlton, remained with cavalry in Alabama until they were paroled.

The questionnaire responses, written in pencil, are legible.

The company roster, given in response to question 45, is not exact. The regimental records include Alfred but not Isaac Stanley; Henry H. but not Tip Taylor; George and Joseph but not Doc Howard; Peyton B. Wheelock, Jr. and Sr. but not Boyd. Nat Borden is not listed on muster rolls for the 5th Regiment and may have been a member of Carter's Scouts.

CHARLTON, JOSEPH E., Pvt (H) 5th (McKenzie's) Tennessee Cavalry Regiment

AKA: Charleton, J. E.
Residence:
Enlisted: December 14, 1861 at Midway, Tennessee by J. B. McLin
Age:

Muster Rolls
Present	1861 Oct 21 - Dec 31	(G - 1st Regt)
Present	1862 Jan - Feb	(G - 1st Regt)
Present	1862 Mar - Apr	(G - 1st Regt)
Present	1862 May - Jun	(Mullendore's Co.)
Present	1862 Jul - Aug	(G - 2nd Bn)
Present	1862 Sep - Oct	(H - 2nd Bn)
Present	1862 Dec 31	(H - 5th Regt)
Present	1863 Jan - Feb	(H - 5th Regt)
Present	1863 Mar - Apr	(H - 5th Regt)
--------	1864 Mar 11 at Tunnel Hill	(Mullendore's Co.)

Transferred June 10, 1863

QUESTIONNAIRE B
[1922]

1. *Name and address:*
   Joseph Edward Charlton, Talbot, Jefferson Co., Tenn.

2. *Age:*
   80 years April 2, 1922.

3. *State and County where born:*
   Tennessee, Sullivan Co.

4. *Confederate or Federal soldier:*
   Confederate.

5. *Name of your Company:*
   Co. H, 5th Tennessee.

6. *Father's occupation.*
   Tailor.

7. *Father's name and details:*
   G. W. Charlton. [Born at] Richmond, Virginia. [Lived at] Bluntville, Sullivan Co., Tenn.

8. *Mother's name and details:*
   Elizabeth Tipton. [Daughter of] John Tipton and [his wife] don't know [who lived] 2 miles Bluntville, Tenn.

9. *Remarks on ancestry:*

10. *Property owned and its value at start of war:*
    No.

11. *Did you or your parents own slaves:*
    No.

12. *Land owned by your parents:*
    No.

13. *Value of property owned by parents:*

14. *Kind of house your parents occupied:*
    Don't remember.

15. *Work you did as boy and young man:*
    Plowed and worked on farm, all kinds of tools.

16. *Work of your father and mother:*
Cooking, weaving, spinning, milking, sewing.

17. *Did your parents keep servants:*
No.

18. *Was honest toil considered respectable:*
Yes.

19. *Did white men engage in such work:*
Yes.

20. *Were there white men idle in your community:*
None. They did the work themselves.

21. *Did slave owners mingle with non-owners:*
Yes.

22. *At gatherings did slaveholders mingle:*
Some.

23. *Was there a friendly feeling between owners and non owners or were slave owners antagonistic:*
No. Some.

24. *Did slaveholders have a political advantage:*
Don't know.

25. *Were opportunities good for poor young men:*
Yes.

26. *Were poor young men encouraged by slave holders:*

27. *What kind of school did you attend:*
Free school.

28. *How long did you go to school:*
Don't remember.

29. *How far to nearest school:*
Near me, in Blountsville, Tenn.

30. *What schools were in your neighborhood:*
Academy and free school.

31. *Was the school private or public:*
Both.

32. *How many months a year did it run:*
    7 to 10 months.

33. *Did boys and girls attend regularly:*
    Yes.

34. *Was the teacher a man or woman:*
    Sometimes both.

35. *When did you enlist:*
    1861, March 1. Limestone Depot, Tenn.

36. *Where was your Company sent first:*
    To Midway, Tenn. to Knoxville, Tenn.

37. *How long before you were engaged in battle:*
    Soon fought bushwhackers in Campbell Co. and Morgan Co.

38. *What was the first battle:*
    Brimstone, Morgan Co., Tenn. All around in Morgan.

39. *Describe your experience in the war:*
    From Kingston to Kentucky, near Lexington. Back to Tenn., near Clinton, Tenn. In battle 4 days at Chickamauga; Mission Ridge; twice Buzzard Roost; Dalton, Ga.; Resaca, Ga.; Calhoun, Ga.; near Cartersville and Marietta, Ga.; then back in Kentucky; on 2 raids to Paris and Richmond, Ky. I was with Carter's scouts 1 yr and 8 months in middle Tenn. At Franklin with Hood. Saw Gen. Cleburne killed at Franklin with saber in his hand.

40. *When and where were you discharged:*

41. *Tell something of your trip home:*

42. *Describe your life after the war:*
    Blacksmith and wood work.

43. *What kind of work did you do after the war:*
    Farmed and blacksmithed; Southern Methodist church; married 19th April 1866; wife was Elizabeth Jett, she is 80 years old during this year.

44. *Tell about some of the great men you have known:*

45. *Names of members of your company:*
    Capt. W. W. Mullendore and
    Capt. Jno. B. Maklin [McLin] was first captain, organized the company.

2nd Lt. Wash Wilcox	Bob Stephens
3rd Lt. Mac B. Broyles	Bill M. Stephens, bugler
Orderly Sgt. D. R. Wilson	Jno. Longmires, 1st Cpl.

Wm. Cannon
Joe Crouch
H. Crouch
Isaac Sampson
Bob Conley
Geo. Smith
Isaac Stanley
Tip [Henry H.] Taylor
Hunter McKlin [McLin]
Sam Blair
Bill Hulse
Jno. King
Doc Howard
Boyd Wheelock
George Kinchelo
Bob McGuin [McGuire?]

Joe Brown
Ike Poor
Andy Kenser [Kincer]
Jack Forman
Asa Hope
Asa Bayless
Mat [Madison] Campbell
John Burson
Wm. Ray [Rhea]
Jim Shefield
Isaac Jackson
Jno. Carson
Eleye [Eldridge] Kinchelo
Nat Borden
Jos. Gibson

Can't remember any more of the co. H names

46. *Names and addresses of any veterans:*
J. E. Myers, Talbot, Tenn.
John Milligan, Jeff. City, Tenn.

I was with Capt. Carter's Scouts. Carter reported to Gen. J. B. Hill at Muffresboro and was on the raid to Nashville. I surrendered to Gen. Thomas at Decatur, Ala. on the 15 day of May 1865.

JOHN FRANKLIN COOLEY

Born March 19, 1832, John F. Cooley was 29 years old when he enlisted in McKenzie's company. He was with the regiment when it was paroled at Charlotte, North Carolina.

The responses to the questionnaire were written in ink and are easily legible. The answer to Question 34 is continued through the next several questions to Question 40.

He did not include a list of Company C but mentioned a few names in response to Question 33. Tom Bogos, listed as 2nd Lieutenant, does not appear on the regimental musters. Green McKenzie may be E. G. McKenzie of Company C who enlisted the same day as Cooley.

COOLEY, JOHN F.; Sgt (C5) 5th (McKenzie's) Tennesee Cavalry Regiment

Residence:	Meigs County
Enlisted:	November 1, 1861 at Decatur by J. W. Gillespie for 12 months in McKenzie's Company
Age:	30 at enlistment; 31 on March 11, 1864 roll
Paroled:	May 3, 1865 at Charlotte, North Carolina

<u>Muster Rolls</u>

Present	1862 Nov 1, 1861 - Feb 28 1862	
Present	1862 Mar - Apr	(B - 1st Regt)
Absent	1862 May - Jun	(C - 2nd Bn)
	At home sick on surgeon's certificate	
	Approved by Col. Morrison June 7, 1862	
Present	1862 Jul - Aug	(B - 2nd Bn)
Present	1862 Sep - Oct	(C - 2nd Bn)
Absent	1862 Nov - Dec	(C - 5th Regt)
	Absent on surgeon's certificate. Approved by	
	Lt. Col. McKenzie November 10, 1862	
Present	1863 Aug 31, 1862 - Feb 28, 1863	(C - 5th Regt)
Present	1863 Mar - Apr	(C - 5th Regt)
	AWOL 27 days	
Present	1863 Mar 11 at Tunnel Hill	(C - 5th Regt)
Present	1864 Dec 31	(C - 5th Regt)

QUESTIONNAIRE A
[1915]

1. *Name and Address:*
   John Franklin Cooley, Bon Air, White Co., Tenn.

2. *Current age:*
   83 years, 19 March 1915.

3. *State and county of birth:*
   Meigs County, Tennessee.

4. *State and county when enlisted:*
   Meigs County, Tennessee.

5. *Occupation before the war:*
   Farming.

6. *Occupation of your father:*
   Farming.

7. *Value of property you owned:*
   Horses, cattle and hogs worth about $200.00.

8. *Slaves owned, if any:*
   None.

9. *Land your parents owned:*
   They owned about fifty acres.

10. *Value of parents' property at onset of war:*
    $500.00. 50 acres land, horses, cattle and hogs.

11. *Kind of house your parents owned:*
    Three log rooms.

12. *What kind of work you did as boy and young man:*
    Plowed, hoed, reeped, and mowed. Most all kind of farm work. Raised corn, wheat, oats, cotton, potatoes, tobacco, cane, rye.

13. *Kind of work your father and mother did:*
    Father did all kinds of work on the farm. Mother and sisters did all the house work, picked cotton, spun, wove and made it into garments and bedding for ourselves and others.

14. *Servants your parents kept, if any:*
    No.

15. *Was honest toil respected in your community:*
    Yes.

16. *Did white men engage in toil:*
    Yes. Some don't do very much hard work. They all men and boys.

17. *Were there white men who idled:*
    None. There were five or six men in our neighborhood owned slaves but they worked with their slaves and were kind to them.

18. *Did slave owners mingle or feel themselves better:*
    All were on an equality. No difference shown.

19. *At public gatherings did slave owners mingle freely:*
    Yes. You couldn't tell them apart if you didn't know it.

20. *Were slave owners and non-owners antagonistic:*
    They were as friendly as men could be.

21. *Did slave owners have a political advantage:*
    No.

22. *Were opportunities good for a poor young man:*
    Yes. The same as at any other time when the man was willing to make the necessary sacrifice and do the work.

23. *Did slave owners encourage or discourage poor young men:*
    Encouraged.

24. *Kind of school you attended:*
    Public schools.

25. *How long did you go to school:*
    About 4 years.

26. *How far was it to the nearest school:*
    A mile.

27. *What schools operated in your neighborhood:*
    The county schools and the Academy at Decatur, Meigs Co., Tenn.

28. *Was your community school private or public:*
    We had both.

29. *How many months a year did it run:*
    The public school ran five months in the year.

30. *Did boys and girls attend regularly:*
    Yes.

31. *Was the teacher a man or a woman:*
    Man.

32. *Year and month you enlisted:*
    In Meigs Co., Tenn. June 1st 1861.

33. *Your Regiment: Members of your company:*
    I first went out in the 1st Tennessee Cavalry for 12 months, then we reinlisted for the war. McLinn our Col. and McKenzie our Lieut. Col.
    W. O. Martin, Captain
    D. C. Blevins, 1st Lt.
    Tom Bogos, 2nd Lt.
    Green McKenzie, Lt.
    five or six Blevins boys

34. *After enlistment where was your company sent:*
    Cross Roads, Rhea County, Tennessee (now Dayton, Tenn.). From there to Knoxville, Tennessee. From there to Cumberland Mt. to guard the mountain passes to keep the enemy from coming through.

35. *How long before your first battle:*
    We were engaged in skirmishing for a year but fought the first big battle at . . .

36. *Your first battle:*
    . . . Chickamauga and then went to Buzzards Roost where we had a battle.

37. *Your experience in the war:*
    We were in skirmishes on to Perryville, living on whatever we could pick up for a month, enduring many hardships. We had a severe battle at Perryville, but captured all the supplies of the enemy and put them to flight but they reinforced and followed us back to Cumberland Gap. The Cavalry remained there some time skirmishing, And at Chickamauga and had a battle there which lasted 3 days and we lost a good many men. We then went back to Tenn. where we had a hard time, enduring much suffering.

38. *When and where discharged:*
    Charlotte, North Carolina, 1st of May 1860 [1865]. . . . After we left Tunnel Hill, Ga., we went to Buzzard Roost. We had several battles on the way. We had another big battle at Kennesaw Mountains and captured about 75 wagons. . .

39. *Describe your trip home:*
    Nothing of importance happened on our way home. . . . We went from Kennesaw to Atlanta, Ga. where we had another big battle. Gen. Hood took charge of the entire army at Atlanta, Ga. After we left Atlanta, we met Capt. [Gen.] Hood at Resaca, Ga. with the entire army where we had a hard fight but failed to take and we went from there to Dalton, Ga. . . .

40. *Describe your work after the war:*
Farming. . . . We had several hard battles after leaving Dalton and on the way to Atlanta and suffered a great deal and we passed from there into North Carolina and to South Carolina. We came to Charlotte, North Carolina. We had several skirmishes about three. I cannot remember all of the battles and incidents connected with them.

41. *A sketch of your life after the war:*
I came from Meigs Co. to Whites Co. in September 1865 and farmed as long as able and have worked at public works since. I obeyed the Gospel of Christ in '74 and have been a member of the Church of God since that time. I was enlisted in the 5th Tenn. Cavalry commanded by G. W. McKenzie. Capt. D. C. Blevins.

42. *Details of your father:*

43. *Details of your mother:*

44. *Remarks on ancestry:*

45. *Name the members of your company:*

46. *Name and address of living veterans:*

JOHN TYLER CRAWFORD

John T. Crawford gave his birthdate as December 31, 1844 and would have been 19 years old when he joined the 5th Regiment on December 10, 1863. However, he gave his enlistment date as June 1861 when he would have been 17. He most likely simply accompanied his father, Capt. John Crawford, when Company E, 26th Infantry, left Rhea County in 1861 but, being underage, was not carried on the rolls.

The responses are neatly typewritten.

The names given in response to Question 45 are members of the infantry company he served with. Of the names listed for Question 46 only W. G. Allen and W. F. Blevins were members of the 5th Regiment.

Crawford gave an account of his adventure with a Yankee in "Experiences Between Sharpshooters" published in the *Confederate Veteran*, Vol. 15 (April 1907), p. 170.

CRAWFORD, J. T.; Pvt (E) 26th Tennessee Infantry Regiment

Enlisted: January 12, 1863 at Tullahoma by Adjt. Hickey for 3 years

Muster Rolls
- Present   1863 Jan - Feb   (E - 26th Regt)
- Present   1863 Mar - Apr   (E - 26th Regt)
- Present   1863 Jul - Aug   (E - 26th Regt)
- Present   1863 Sep - Oct   (E - 26th Regt)
- --------   1864 Jan 26 at Dalton (James A. Cash's Co.)
    Age as 18
- --------   1864 Jan - Feb   (E - 26th Regt)
    Transferred to the 5th Tenn Cav by order of Gen'l ------

CRAWFORD, J. T.; Pvt (D) 5th (McKenzie's) Tennessee Cavalry Regiment

AKA: Crawford, J. T.
Residence: Washington, Rhea County
Enlisted: January 12, 1863 at Tullahoma by A. C. Hickey
Age: 16 on March 11, 1864 roll
Paroled: May 3, 1865 at Charlotte, North Carolina

Muster Rolls
- ---------   1864 Mar 11   (D - 5th Regt)
    Transferred December 10, 1863
- Absent   1864 Nov - Dec   (D - 5th Regt)
    Absent sick near Jonesboro, Tennessee, December 3, 1864 with small pox
- POW   1864 Aug 24
    W. W. Wright, Lt. Commdg prison received J.T. Crawford of Rhea County, 5th Tenn Cav at Chattanooga as a prisoner

QUESTIONNAIRE B
[1922]

1. *Name and address:*
   John Tyler Crawford, Tyler, Texas

2. *Age:*
   77 years. Born Dec 31, 1844.

3. *State and County where born:*
   Born Rhea County, Tenn.

4. *Confederate or Federal soldier:*
   Confederate.

5. *Name of your company:*
   Company E, 26th Tenn Infantry and Company D, 5th Tenn Cavalry. Transfer and parole in my possession.

6. *Father's occupation:*
   Farmer and stock trader.

7. *Father's name and details:*
   John Crawford, [*Born*] on North Holston River, Washington County, Tenn. December 10th 1808. [*Lived*] near Washington, Rhea County, Tenn. Was J.P., tax assessor, Capt. Co. E, 26th Tenn Infantry. Captured at Ft. Donelson and died in Indianapolis after being taken out of prison by Masons and Sheriff Johnson of Indianapolis in whose home he died.

8. *Mother's name and details:*
   Martha Griffith, [*Born*] in Grainger County, Tenn in 1810. Daughter of Levi Griffith and [*his wife*] Jane Shelton Griffith [*who lived*] in Tennessee Valley just north of where Dayton now is.

9. *Remarks on ancestry:*
   Great grandfather John Crawford, born at Staunton, Va. Oct 21, 1762. Enlisted 3 times in Colonial service, Revolutionary War. From Surry County, N.C., first under Capt. Smith and Col. Matthew Locke, 2nd time under Capt. Gibson Woolright and Maj. Joel Lewis, 3rd time under Capt. Edmund Hickman & Col. Rutherford. Engaged in Battles of Brier Creek & Eutaw Springs. Moved to Washington County, Tenn. His eldest son, William A. (my grandfather), born Sept. 2, 1783 married Martha Blakely, moved to Hamilton County, Tenn. near present site of Chattanooga, and died there Sept 15th 1834. He had eleven children, one among the youngest being my father, John Crawford, who moved with him down the Tenn River on a flatboat to Ross' Landing and later moved to Rhea County. Grandfather Griffith was in war of 1812 and went from fort on Hiwassee River to New Orleans in flatboat, arriving there just after the battle.

10. *Property owned and its value at start of war:*
    Was a boy of only sixteen years and had no property except a pony, a dog, and a gun.

11. *Did your parents own slaves:*
Yes, four.

12. *Land owned by your parents:*
350 acres in Rhea County and tract in Bradley County.

13. *Value of property owned by parents:*
In land, horses (he had many horses), slaves, and other property $30,000.00.

14. *Kind of house your parents occupied:*
Two large two story hewed log front with wide hall and one story frame two room L for dining room and kitchen. Large brick fireplaces and chimneys. House still standing and in good condition.

15. *Work you did as boy and young man:*
Any and all kinds of work necessary to be done, was an expert with mowing blade and fork. Also in binding grain and stacking wheat or hay. Never was good plowman or driver of team. Had a brother who was considered best horseman in the county. He died in Confederate service. I left the farm to join the army and was on farm only a short time after the war.

16. *Work of your father and mother:*
Father was a farmer and stock trader. Bought and sold horses and mules, driving them south. Also bought and sold hogs. I had three sisters about grown and my mother worked only as she wanted to. My grandmother Griffith lived with us after her husband's death and, being a splendid hand at spinning, knitting, sewing and fancy quilt work, she and my mother engaged in this a great deal of the time.

17. *Did your parents keep servants:*
Yes, three men on the farm and an old negro woman, "Aunt Delphia," who helped around the house some.

18. *Was honest toil considered respectable:*
Yes, all the boys in our neighborhood worked on the farm when not in school. Idleness was not tolerated. Most all land owners lived on their farms and cultivated them. If they had slaves they would work them, but their sons, if they had any, also worked. There were no profligates in Rhea County.

19. *Did white man engage in such work:*
See statement above.

20. *Were white men idle:*
As stated above, there were very few if any in this section of Tenn.

21. *Did slave owners mingle with non-owners:*
Mingled freely without any perceptible difference. No class distinction between honest, industrious families.

22. *At gatherings did slaveholders mingle:*
    No distinction whatever as long as character warranted.

23. *Were slaveholders friendly or antagonistic:*
    Associations were very cordial.

24. *Did slaveholders have a political advantage.*
    No.

25. *Were opportunities good for poor young men:*
    Yes, and the rule was that such opportunities were usually taken advantage of.

26. *Were poor young men encouraged by slave holders:*
    Encouraged and helped always.

27. *What kind of school did you attend:*
    From seven to fourteen I attended the common school three months each year. Fourteen to sixteen Washington Academy.

28. *How long did you go to school:*
    Perhaps about three years and eight months if all added together.

29. *How far to nearest school:*
    Half mile to common school and 2 1/2 miles to the Washington Academy.

30. *What schools were in your neighborhood:*
    The above named Washington Academy was a very fine institution in its day. Its instructors were graduates from colleges and universities and were very thorough in their work.

31. *Was the school public or private:*
    Common, public; academy, private.

32. *How many months a year did it run:*
    Public 3 to 4 months, Washington Academy ten months.

33. *Did boys and girls attend regularly:*
    Yes, as a rule.

34. *Was the teacher a man or woman:*
    Most often a man. Sometimes a woman. Always a man as principal in the academy.

35. *When did you enlist:*
    June 1861 at Washington, Tenn. in the Confederate Army.

36. *Where was your Company sent first:*
    To Knoxville, Tenn. where the 26th Tenn Regt was organized, my Co. being Co. E. To Bowling Green, thence to Ft. Donelson.

37. *How long before you were engaged in battle:*
From June 1861 to Feb 1862, or less than seven months.

38. *What was the first battle:*
Murfreesboro. (I was left at Bowling Green with "mumps" and was not at Ft. Donelson where my father was captured).

39. *Describe your experience in the war:*
From Murfreesboro to Tullahoma for balance of winter '63. No soldier who saw service in '61 to '65 as I did could put one tenth in this space. Was in battle at Chickamauga and Lookout Mountain and Missionary Ridge. In several small engagements. Captured once but escaped. Was transferred to the 5th Tenn Cavalry and with them during Ga. Campaign, Dalton to Atlanta. Was with Vaughn's cavalry from Sept. 1864 to March 1865. In two of his fights at Rogersville and Bull Gap. Returned to Wheeler's cavalry with Col. McKenzie, reaching Greensboro, N.C. just before Lee surrendered. Was at Confedt Hdqrs until Johnson surrendered. Left Greensboro to be paroled with command. Was paroled at Charlotte, N.C. in April 1865.

40. *When and where were you discharged:*

41. *Tell something of your trip home:*
Trip home made on horseback, through N.C. via Ashville down French Broad through Sevierville and Maryville where a splendid breakfast was furnished us at the request of Adjt. Hood of Jim Brownlow's 2nd Tenn Federal Regt. Confdt troops returning this route, as I remember, were 2nd E. Tenn, Col. Coon; 5th Tenn, Col. McKenzie; 9th Tenn Bat., Col. Aiken; and possibly 4th Tenn.

42. *Describe your life after the war:*
Planted corn in May '65. Had lost my father, mother, and one brother during the war, and with my oldest brother and four sisters settled down to farming as best we could. All stock except one colt had been taken by Yankees, and few tools were left but we managed to make enough to do the family.

43. *What kind of work did you do after the war:*
Left the farm in Dec 1866 and went as a clerk on the steamboat "Cherokee," plying between Chattanooga and Knoxville. Continued on the river as clerk, pilot and master for twelve years. Married Captain John Doss' daughter, Mary Kate, Dec 25, 1867.

Carried on farming just below Kingston in connection with steamboating until 1879 when we sold out and moved to Crystal Falls, Texas. Went into mercantile business there but sold out and went into cattle business. Sold out at Crystal Falls and moved to Weatherford and went with T. P. Railroad. With them seven years. Moved from Weatherford to Pampa, Gray Co., where I now live. In sheriff's two years. Organized a Hail Insurance Co. a number of years ago and have been its secretary ever since. Have held offices as Chmn. Ex. Com. Texas State Alliance, census enumerator, and several other unimportant offices.

Was personally acquainted with Andrew Johnson, Gov. Isham G. Harris, Gov. John C. Brown, Robt L. Taylor, and was slightly acquainted with your present Gov. Alf Taylor. Was detailed for a short time during '64 on Gen. Joe Wheeler's secret service and became intimately acquainted with him just after the war. Knew from my boyhood Postmaster D. M. Key and was personally acquainted with Horace Maynard and U. S. Judge Baxter. Since moving to Texas was a fellow townsman of Ex. Gov. Samuel T. Lanham and know Ex. Gov. Jas. S. Hogg.

44. *Tell about some of the great men you have known:*

45. *Names of members of your company:*
Company "E," 26th Tennessee Infantry Regiment

John Crawford	Captain
Dr. A. C. Blevins	1st Lieut.
J. A. Howell	2nd "
Hannibal Paine	3rd "
James Johnson	1st Sergent
George P. Roddy	2nd "
H. A. Crawford	3rd "
James Flemming	4th "
J. A. Cash	1st Corp
G. R. Todd	2nd "
Columbus Gibson	3rd "
John Majors	4th "

By referring to "Rhea and Meigs Counties in the Confederate War" by Col. V. C. Allen, you will find a full roster of not only Company E, but also the seven or eight other companies organized in Rhea and Meigs Counties. Doubtless this book can be secured from W. G. Allen, Dayton, Tenn.

46. *Names and addresses of any veterans:*

Capt.	George Brown	Dallas	Texas
"	Wm. Gaston	"	"
	Val Work	"	"
	Wm. Work	"	"
	J. T. Benton	Pampa	"
	C. W. Saunders	"	"
	Uriah Hayes	White Deer	"
	E. N. Gannaway	Dayton	Tenn
	James Jewell	"	"
	J. H. Jewell	"	"
	Ace Johnson	"	"
	W. G. Allen	"	"
	Rev. G. W. Brewer	"	"
	W. F. Blevins	"	"
	W. P. Thomison	" R 4	"
	Ark Whittle	"	"
	E. S. Larmer	"	"
	T. J. Robinson	Evensville	Tenn
	H. Jennoe	Dayton R 1	"
	I. K. Brown	" R 1	"

WILLIAM OWEN DAVIS

Born November 18, 1837, W. O. Davis was 23 at the time of his enlistment in McKenzie's company. Apparently he became too ill to continue serving and was not with the regiment at the time of its surrender. According to his headstone in Walnut Grove Cemetery (Meigs County), William died on June 11, 1932. His wife, Eliza Louise Spradling (March 29, 1846 - April 10, 1932), and brother, Tennessee A. Davis (born September 1843), are in the same cemetery. T.A.'s stone has "Co C, 5th Tenn Cav CSA."

The responses, written in pencil, were omitted for most of the questions.

The partial list of Company C, given in response to Question 45, includes Bedney Davis who does not appear on regimental rolls; Temmie Davis may be T. A. Davis, Rodney Blevins may be R. E. L. Blevins and blank Nance may be J. C. Nance. Others on the list can be identified as members of the company.

DAVIS, WILLIAM O.; Pvt. (C5) 5th (McKenzie's) Tennessee Cavalry Regiment

Residence:
Enlisted: March 10, 1862 at Fincastle by Capt. McKenzie
Age: 25 on March 11, 1864 roll

Muster Rolls

--------	1862 Nov 1, 1861 - Feb 28 (dated Apr 8, 1862)	(B - 1st Regt)
Present	1862 Mar - Apr	(B - 1st Regt)
Present	1862 May - Jun	(C - 2nd Bn)
Absent	1862 Jul - Aug	(B - 2nd Bn)

At home on surgeon's certificate. Approved by Col. McLin July 20, 1862

Present	1862 Sep - Oct	(C - 2nd Bn)
Present	1862 Nov - Dec	(C - 5th Regt)
Present	1863 Aug 31, 1862 - Feb 28	(C - 5th Regt)
Present	1863 Mar - Apr	(C - 5th Regt)
--------	1864 Mar 11 at Tunnel Hill	(C - 5th Regt)

AWOL since November 1, 1863

Absent	1864 Dec 31	(C - 5th Regt)

Absent. Left sick in East Tennessee

QUESTIONNAIRE B
April 1922

1. *Name and address:*
   William Owen Davis, R.F.D. #1, Box #16, Decatur, Tenn.

2. *Age:*
   84 years the 18 of last November.

3. *State and County where born:*
   State of Tenn., Meigs Co.

4. *Confederate or Federal soldier:*
   Confederate soldier.

5. *Name of your Company:*
   Co. C.

6. *Father's occupation.*
   A loom maker and shoe maker.

7. *Father's name and details:*
   John Davis.

8. *Mother's name and details:*
   Nancy Adams. [*Daughter of*] Sam Adams, Betsey Adams.

9. *Remarks on ancestry:*

10. *Property owned and its value at start of war:*
    One horse worth $150.00 and some hogs worth about $15.00.

11. *Did you or your parents own slaves:*
    Neither one owned any.

12. *Land owned by your parents:*
    About two hundred acres.

13. *Value of property owned by parents:*
    About $7,000.00.

14. *Kind of house your parents occupied:*
    A log house with four rooms.

15. *Work you did as boy and young man:*
    I plowed with a wooden stock plow and a bull tongue plow and used a weeding hoe made in a shop.

16. *Work of your father and mother:*

17. *Did your parents keep servants:*

18. *Was honest toil considered respectable:*

19. *Did white men engage in such work:*

20. *Were white men idle:*

21. *Did slave owners mingle with non-owners:*

22. *At gatherings did slaveholders mingle:*

23. *Were slaveholders friendly or antagonistic:*

24. *Did slaveholders have a political advantage:*

25. *Were opportunities good for poor young men:*

26. *Were poor young men encouraged by slave holders:*

27. *What kind of school did you attend:*

28. *How long did you go to school:*

29. *How far to nearest school:*

30. *What schools were in your neighborhood:*

31. *Was the school private or public:*

32. *How many months a year did it run:*

33. *Did boys and girls attend regularly:*

34. *Was the teacher a man or woman:*

35. *When did you enlist:*

36. *Where was your Company sent first:*

37. *How long before you were engaged in battle:*

38. *What was the first battle:*

39. *Describe your experience in the war:*

40. *When and where were you discharged:*

41. *Tell something of your trip home.*

42. *Describe your life after the war:*

43. *What kind of work did you do after the war:*

44. *Tell about some of the great men you have known:*

45. *Names of members of your company:*
   Dave Blevins
   Bedney Davis
   John Lewis
   Temmie Davis
   Jim Lewis
   Rodney Blevins
   Jim Lillard
   Frank Gwinn
   Blank Nance
   Joe Hampton
   Eligah Gregory
   John Owens

46. *Names and addresses of any veterans:*

D. FRANK DUCKWORTH

D. Frank Duckworth's service record shows that he enlisted in the 5th Regiment on April 16, 1864 at Tunnel Hill but he states in the response to Question 37 that he served under Gen. Forrest until after the battle of Chickamauga, having enlisted in August 1861 at Rhea Springs. Company B (Capt. Bert Leuty) of the 3rd (Brazelton's) Tennessee Cavalry Battalion, later Company A in 1st (Carter's) Tennessee Cavalry Regiment was organized in August 1861 at Sulphur (Rhea) Springs but no prior record has been found for Frank Duckworth in this or any other unit. John Duckworth, also of Company B, 5th Regiment, who may have been a relative, transferred from the 3rd (Carter's) Battalion to the 5th Regiment on August 8, 1862.

The response is in ink in excellent handwriting and probably copied by someone other than the respondent.

The men listed in response to Question 33 can be identified as members of Company B with the exception of Bratch Johnson who may have been F. L. B. Johnson.

DUCKWORTH, D. F.; Pvt (B) 5th (McKenzie's) Tennessee Cavalry Regiment

Residence: Decatur, Meigs County
Enlisted: April 16, 1864 at Tunnel Hill, Georgia by Capt. Blythe for the war
Age:
Paroled: May 3, 1865 at Charlotte, North Carolina

<u>Muster Rolls</u>
Present   1864 Nov - Dec   (B - 5th Regt)

QUESTIONNAIRE A
[1922]

1. *Name and address:*
   D. Frank Duckworth, Blackford Street, Chattanooga, Tenn.

2. *Current age:*
   72.

3. *State and county of birth:*
   Tennessee, Rhea County.

4. *State and county when enlisted:*
   Rhea County, Tenn.

5. *Occupation before the war:*
   Farmer.

6. *Occupation of your father:*

7. *Value of property you owned:*
   None.

8. *Slaves owned, if any:*
   No.

9. *Land your parents owned:*
   Eighty acres.

10. *Value of parents' property at onset of war:*
    $1,500.00.

11. *Kind of house your parents owned:*
    Log house, two rooms.

12. *What kind of work you did as boy and young man:*
    All kinds of farm work.

13. *Kind of work your father and mother did:*
    My father done all kinds of farm work and my mother attended to all of the household duties.

14. *Servants your parents kept, if any:*
    No.

15. *Was honest toil respected in your community:*
    Yes.

16. *Did white men engage in toil:*
    Yes.

17. *Did white men idle while others worked:*
    All the white men in Rhea County worked and worked hard from sunup to sundown.

18. *Did slave ownmers mingle or feel themselves better:*
    All slave owners in our community mixed and mingled with the non-slave owners and it is untrue that they thought themselves better than anyone else.

19. *At public gatherings did slave owners mingle freely:*
    Yes.

20. *Were slave owners and non-owners antagonistic:*
    Friendly.

21. *Did slave owners have a political advantage:*
    No.

22. *Were opportunities good for a poor young man:*
    Yes.

23. *Did slave owners encourage or discourage poor young men:*
    Encouraged.

24. *Kind of school you attended:*
    Country school.

25. *How long did you go to school:*
    About six months.

26. *How far was it to the nearest school:*
    Two miles.

27. *What schools operated in your neighborhood:*
    One country school.

28. *Was your community school private or public:*
    Public.

29. *How many months a year did it run:*
    Three months.

30. *Did boys and girls attend regularly:*
    Fairly well.

31. *Was the teacher a man or a woman:*
Man.

32. *Year and month you enlisted:*
In August 1861, Rhea Springs, Tenn.

33. *Your Regiment: Members of your company:*
Fifth Tenn. Regiment.
> Capt. John Blythe
> Bratch Johnson
> Jim Guffey
> Jos. Pearson
> Carter Guffey
> Sam Guffey
> Carter Lathram [Latham]
> Tom Lathram [Latham]
> Tom Hood
> Tom Smith

34. *After enlistmet where was your company sent:*
Knoxville, Tennessee.

35. *How long before your first battle:*
About six months.

36. *Your first battle:*
Fishing Creek, Ky.

37. *Your experiences in the war:*
During the war I was first under Gen. Forrest until the Battle of Chickamauga. Was under Gen. Joe Wheeler, Ashby's Brigade, Humes' Division, Wheeler's Corps.

In answer to your question number 37, will state that after the battle of Fishing Creek, Kentucky, our regiment went to Cumberland Gap and, outside of a few skirmishes, we were not in a real battle again until the battle of Chicamauga which lasted three days. And as I remember, my company contained at that time one hundred and four men. And after this battle only thirty were left. During this time we had very little to eat and were very thinly clad and slept mostly rolled up in a blanket on the ground, as we had no tents.

After the battle of Chicamauga we went from Chattanooga to Smith's Crossing which is now Dayton, Tennessee, crossed Walden's Ridge at that point to Dunlap and from there to McMinnville. It took us four days to make this trip and during that time we were without both food and shelter. We were in a skirmish at McMinnville and captured four regiments of Yankees and on Duck River, just beyond McMinnville, we had one day of hard fighting. After leaving Duck River we went to Muscle Shoals and forded the river there and came back to Chattanooga, and engaged in the battle of Missionary Ridge.

After the battle of Missionary Ridge we went from there to New Hope Church, Georgia, where we were engaged in battle lasting about one day and from there to Resacca, Ga. and from Resacca to Kenesaw Mountains. We engaged in the battle of Peachtree which lasted about two days to the best of my memory. From then on were engaged in battles in North Carolina and finally surrendered at Charlotte, N.C. in May 1865.

38. *When and where discharged:*
Charlotte, N.C. May 1865.

39. *Describe your trip home:*
I rode my horse home, taking eight days, averaging about one meal per day on way.

40. *Describe your work after war:*
Went to Texas and picked cotton for two years and drove cattle the next three.

41. *A sketch of your life after the war:*
Have been engaged as common laborer ever since.

42. *Name and details of your father:*
John Duckworth. [*Born*] North Carolina; don't know [*County*]. [*Lived in*] N. C.

43. *Name and details of your mother:*
Rebecca Snow. [*Daughter of*] Larkin Snow and [*his wife*] don't know. [*Lived in*] N.C.

44. *Remarks on ancestry:*
Don't know.

45. *Name the members of your company:*

46. *Name and address of living veterans:*

WILLIAM CLENTON GODSEY

Godsey returned both questionnaires, but one is incorrectly filed in the Archives under the name "N. C. Godsey." Form A was completed in pencil and is faded and stained but legible. The responses to Form B are typewritten. Apparently the typist, working from handwritten material could not read some words and left blanks in the response to Question 39 of Form B.

Company I was organized July 19, 1862 by Capt. W. W. Lillard who had served in Company D. as a lieutenant. In answer to Question 35, Form B, Godsey stated that he enlisted July 1862 at Shiloh Church, Meigs County, but to Question 32, Form A, he gave "the last of sixty-two at Decatur . . . in a company that went out in July before. The company was at Knoxville when I went." This latter statement indicates that the company had already returned from Bragg's foray into Kentucky when he joined it. His service record gives his enlistment date as February 13, 1863.

Another puzzling statement by Godsey is in response to Question 39, Form B where he states: "Company I was with Fifth Tennessee Cavalry as rear guard from Perryville through Cumberland Gap into Tennessee. Then we went to Murfreesboro, was engaged in that fearful contest." The Battle of Murfreesboro took place December 31, 1862 to January 2, 1863. Some records indicate that all the cavalry except the 5th Tennessee was withdrawn from East Tennessee and sent to Bragg's support at Murfreesboro. There is no record of the 5th Regiment having participated in that battle. Some of the companies were in surrounding counties, rounding up conscripts, but a detachment of the regiment, under command of Col. G. W. McKenzie, may well have been at Murfreesboro.

Born September 10, 1844, William Godsey would have been 19 years old on February 13, 1863. He served the remainder of the war and was paroled with the regiment. William died on October 28, 1924, and was buried in Buttram Cemetery in Dayton, Tennessee.

Of the list of veterans given in response to Question 46, Form B, Nute Molton, Thomas Neal, and Jerome King do not appear on the 5th Regiment muster rolls.

GODSEY, WILLIAM C.; Pvt (I) 5th (McKenzie's) Tennessee Cavalry Regiment

Residence: Meigs County
Enlisted: February 13, 1863 at Decatur by D. C. Blevins for 3 years
Age: 21 on March 11, 1864 roll
Paroled: May 3, 1865 at Charlotte, North Carolina

Muster Rolls
Present   1863 Feb 28   (I - 5th Regt)
Present   1863 Mar - Apr   (I - 5th Regt)
--------   1864 Mar 11 at Tunnel Hill   (Lillard's Co.)
Present   1864 Nov - Dec   (I - 5th Regt)

QUESTIONNAIRE A
[1915]

1. *Name and Address:*
   W. C. Godsey, Dayton, Tenn. Star Route to Big Spring Road.

2. *Current age:*
   Seventy years twentyeth of last Sept. 1914.

3. *State and county of birth:*
   Tenn. Rhea County but moved -- now live Meigs Co.

4. *State and county when enlisted:*
   Tennessee.

5. *Occupation before the war:*
   Farming.

6. *Occupation of your father:*
   Farming.

7. *Value of property you owned:*
   I wasn't of age even when the war closed. My mother was a widow and our farm lay on the Tennessee River, the farm where I now live, 220 acres. However, I own that now and more. I have lived on this since I was four years old except during the war, three years with the 5th Tenn. Cavalry, Col. G. W. McKenzie.

8. *Slaves owned, if any:*
   Six. Two negro women, one negro man and three negro children.

9. *Land your parents owned:*
   220. The place where I now live in Meigs County, Tennessee.

10. *Value of parents' property at onset of war:*
    Our land would have brought about three thousand dollars. We had plenty of stock, tools to run the farm, value one thousand dollars, value of negroes about six thousand dollars.

11. *Kind of house your parents owned:*
    We lived in two story log house, another log house for stove and table and another for the negroes thirty yards away, and still another, a log house, stove and dirt floor in the negro kitchen. I learned to dance with visiting negroes.

12. *What kind of work you did as boy and young man:*
    I worked at all kinds of farm work. Raked hay with wooden toothed rake, also with two pronged wooden fork. I worked with the negro men and eat the same kind of diet.

13. *Kind of work your father and mother did:*
    My father done field work, also turned land with yoke of streers and old McCormick plow. Sometimes I had to drive them and I would fall down more times than I would stand. My mother worked at all kinds of house work. She was stout and there [wasn't] any kind of house work she couldn't do. She wove all kinds of coverlids and counterpanes, three and four tredel twilled blankets and all other kinds.

14. *Servants your parents kept, if any:*
    One of the negro women kept the kitchen except washday. Mother took the kitchen and a sister helped at the wash place.

15. *Was honest toil respected in your community?*
    I don't remember hearing such discussed but do remember them that had no trade or occupation didn't stand well with the old folks. Nothing much but farming was carried on in my community at that time.

16. *Did white men engage in toil:*
    They all worked some. Nothing much but farming was going on in our community.

17. *Did white men idle while others worked:*
    This was new country and all worked some.

18. *Did slave owners mingle or feel themselves better:*
    We were more thinly settled then than we are now and more to visit then than now. When there was a gathering we would have more visitors than stables and we would have horses tied in dozens fence corners, eating bundled oats and fodder.

19. *At public gatherings did slave owners mingle freely:*
    Entirely so. All wore home made clothes and mingled together and you couldn't tell one from the other, only knowing them at home.

20. *Were slave owners and non-owners antagonistic:*
    I knew of no malice or prejudice on account of slaves.

21. *Did slave owners have a political advantage:*
    Slaves was no part of qualifications for office, neither was they a disbarment.

22. *Were opportunities good for a poor young man:*
    In those days money was scarce in these parts and good openings for young men were scarce owing to this being entirely farming community and no railroads to ship produce.

23. *Did slave owners encourage or discourage poor young men:*
    They got all the encouragement that could be extended in our conditions.

24. *Kind of school you attended:*
    Public and subscription.

25. *How long did you go to school:*

26. *How far was it to the nearest school:*
Godsey's School House was on our place.

27. *What schools operated in your neighborhood:*
Small neighborhood schools.

28. *Was your community school private or public:*
Both, but the trouble we pulled fodder and picked peas and beans.

29. *How many months a year did it run:*
The schools run two and a half to three months each year but in each year we pulled fodder and chilled [shelled peas?] most of the school periods and got about the same distance in our books each year.

30. *Did boys and girls attend regularly:*

31. *Was the teacher a man or a woman:*
Men all public schools. Sometimes a young lady would teach a little spring school.

32. *Year and month you enlisted:*
About the last [of eighteen] sixty-two at Decatur, the county seat of my county, in a company that went out in July before. The company was at Knoxville when I went.

33. *Your Regiment: Members of your company:*
5th Tenn. McKenzie's Regiment who also went from this county. I could give the names of each member that served with my company. Our officers was Capt. W.W. Lillard, Jesse Martin, J.M. McKinzey, W.F. Blevins. Commissioned officers. We went from Meigs Co. to Chattanooga. Gen. Bragg was preparing to go into Ky. Capt. Lillard was ordered to Sparta, Tenn., reported to Lt. Col. Combs.[36] At Sparta, Capt. Lillard became Gen. Bragg's escort and dispatch bearer. At Perryville every man of the company was bearing dispatches. After the Perryville battle we took our place as Co. I, 5th Tenn. Cav.

34. *After enlistment where was your company sent:*
We went to Scott County and to keep down the bushwhackers. We done scout and picket duty for several months.

35. *How long before your first battle:*
We were in some kind of skirmish almost every day or surely every week. Our first hard battle was at Perryville, then Chickamauga, New Hope Church.

36. *Your first battle:*
Perryville, Ky.

37. *Your experience in the war:*
After Perryville Battle we came to E. Tenn. Did duty under Col. J.S. Scott as Brigade Commander. Made two raids into Ky. Fought two battles at Big Hill to Battle [two battles] at Richmond and had many skirmishes. Then to Chickamauga. Then Johnston from Dalton to Atlanta. Then Wheeler through Tenn. and back to Georgia to Savannah. From Savannah to Bentonville. The 19th of March we fought our last battle. We fought in some way nearly every day, sometimes nearly naked, sometimes very hungry, never a tent to sleep.

38. *When and where discharged:*
Near Charlotte, N.C. under Gen'l Jo Wheeler on 29th day of April 1865.

39. *Describe your trip home:*
On 4th of May we succeeded in getting rations[?] and food to last us three days. After passing Ashville at the gap of the mountain as you come down into Wautaugah valley one Col. Kirk stopped us, would pay no attention to our parole, ordered us to give up our horses. After much parley and insult, Col. McKenzie ordered his officers who had side arms to form a line and force our passage. 14 officers had pistols and rode forward to make a charge on Col. Kirk's regiment of desperados. They saw some of them would be killed and opened up the way and we passed.

40. *Describe your work after the war:*

41. *A sketch of your life after the war:*

42. *Details of your father:*

43. *Details of your mother:*

44. *Remarks on ancestry:*

45. *Name the members of your company:*

46. *Name and address of living veterans:*

QUESTIONNAIRE B
[1922]

1. *Name and address:*
   William Clenton Godsey, Dayton, Tennessee.

2. *Age:*
   77 years old, Sept. 1921.

3. *State and County where born:*
   Rhea County, State of Tennessee.

4. *Confederate or Federal soldier:*
   I was a Confederate soldier.

5. *Name of your Company:*
   Co. I, 5th Tenn.

6. *Father's occupation:*
   Farmer.

7. *Father's name and details:*
   Stephen Jett Godsey. [*Born*] Scott Co. Virginia, moved to Hawkins County, Tenn.

8. *Mother's name and details:*
   Mary Gibbons. [*Daughter of*] John Gibbons. Don't know given name of grandmother.

9. *Remarks on ancestry:*
   I have no records showing that they were Revolutionary War. I have heard Mother say they were Tories. My great grandparents came from Ireland, I don't know the dates.

10. *Property owned and its value at start of war:*
    I did not own any property time of the war. I was just a boy.

11. *Did you or your parents own slaves:*
    My parents owned six slaves.

12. *Land owned by your parents:*
    My parents owned 220 acres of land.

13. *Value of property owned by parents:*
    Ten Thousand Dollars.

14. *Kind of house your parents occupied:*
    It was a hewed log house, three rooms.

15. *Work you did as boy and young man:*
    I did all kinds of farm work.

16. *Work of your father and mother:*
    Father was a good farmer, could do all kinds of work. My mother was a great weaver, weaving all kinds of blankets, coverlids and spinning and weaving us children all of our wear. I have a coverlid she wove, a counterpane heavier than a blanket.

17. *Did your parents keep servants:*
    Kept none but their negroes.

18. *Was honest toil considerd respectable:*
    All kinds of labor was regarded as honorable.

19. *Did white men engage in such work:*
    All respectable men engaged in such work.

20. *Were white men idle:*
    All persons leading idle lives were ignored by society.

21. *Did slave owners mingle with non-owners.*
    All respectable men mingled socially, slave owners and [non] slave holders.

22. *At gatherings did slaveholders mingle:*
    Negroes did not go to school with white children, but at Good Hope Church, in Meigs County, they would come to Church.

23. *Was there a friendly feeling between slave owners and non owners:*
    There was.

24. *Did slaveholders have a political advantage:*
    The man that was needy got the best support:

25. *Were opportunities good for poor young men:*
    They were not very good, money being scarce.

26. *Were poor young men encouraged by slave holders:*
    They were encouraged.

27. *What kind of school did you attend:*
    The public schools of that day.

28. *How long did you go to school:*
    I probably attended school eighteen months.

29. *How far to nearest school:*
    It was nearby on Father's land.

30. *What schools were in your neighborhood:*
Nothing but public schools.

31. *Was the school private or public:*
It was public.

32. *How many months a year did it run:*
About three months.

33. *Did boys and girls attend regularly:*
They were not overly attended.

34. *Was the teacher a man or woman:*
They were all male.

35. *When did you enlist:*
In July 1862, at Shiloh Church, Meigs County.

36. *Where was your Company sent first:*
To Chattanooga. Reported to Gen. Bragg.

37. *How long before you were engaged in battle:*
Oct 8, at Perryville.

38. *What was the first battle:*
Perryville.

39. *Describe your experiences in the war.*
Company "I" was with Fifth Tennessee Cavalry as rear guard from Perryville through Cumberland Gap into Tennessee. Then we went to Murfreesboro, was engaged in that fearful contest. Then we were ordered back into East Tennessee, had many skirmishes with bushwhackers all over East Tennessee and Kentucky mountains. Made four raids into Kentucky, fought 4 battles at Crab Orchard, Big Hill, Stanton, Richmond and Paris and other Kentucky towns.

August 20, 1863, Burnside drove us from Big Creek Gap and the 5th Tenn. Cavalry became rear guard of all troops evacuating East Tennessee till we reached Hiwassee River. Then we were placed as pickets on Bragg's right from Orchard Knob to Tennessee River. The 6th of September we were ordered to Ringgold and fought Wilder for 12 days till the 19th of Sept. and forced Wilder and Mitchell back on the Ringgold and Chattanooga [road] on the 20th of Sept.

We were on Missionary Ridge when Gen. Wheeler made his Tennessee raid and destroyed the Federal supplies in Sequatchie Valley. Then to Farmington where our regiment lost 70 men in 30 minutes. Into Alabama, back to Bragg, and had no tents, poor beef, rice crackers for our daily rations, one of the hardest winters I ever experienced. We did picket duty all winter at Tunnel Hill save 30 days we went to Cave Spring to recuperate our horses. Then back on rear guard picket duty till Bragg was relieved and Gen. Johnston became our commander.

Then I was in all the engagements for Johnston, 120 days, fight in and around Atlanta to Jonesboro then to _____ river above Macon. Recuperated and shod horses for 10 days, then with Gen. Wheeler on another raid into Tennessee and around the Federal Army back into Dalton, Ga. and then to North Alabama, then, and here we had a hard fight with a brigade of drunk negroes, fought many raiding parties Sherman sent out into Ga.

Then we crossed the Savannah River and done pickett duty one month, 15 miles above city of Savannah when Gen. Johnston reorganized the shattered regiment, we were in his rear on to the ___ of ____ and to the 19th of March 1865 when we fought our last battle at Bentonville, N.C. when Johnston and Sherman came to terms of surrender. We were parolled on April 29th and Gen. Wheeler bid us adieu. Sherman and Johnston's terms allowed us our officers to keep their side arms and horses.

The 4th day of May 1865 we started for home by way of Ashville, N.C. At the head of the Watauga Mountain where the road enters a narrow gap, one Col. Kirk with 300 or more men lined up and demanded our arms and horses. After a long parley, the Col. told Adj. Allen to bring up the officers as they were all that had pistols. There were 14 of them and Col. Kirk was told to open ranks and let us pass or somebody would be killed. He opened up a way through his robbing and murderous gang and [we] proceeded, arriving at home about the 10th of May 1865.

40. *When and where were you discharged:*

41. *Tell something of your trip home:*

42. *Describe your life after the war:*
Farm work.

43. *What kind of work did you do after the war:*
I am a Baptist. I was a member of the Good Hope Baptist until I moved.

44. *Tell about some of the great men you have known:*
I have seen Gen. Bragg, Gen. Johnston, Gen. Wheeler, Gen. Bates, Gen. Brown as soldiers and Bates, Brown, Harris, Andy Johnston as Governors. I have seen Jennings Bryant, one of our smartest men, and many great divines, J.R. Graves and Billy Sunday.

45. *Names of members of your company:*
    J. M. McKenzie   Big Spring, Meigs County, Tenn.
    W. F. Blevins   Dayton, Tenn.
    Hiram Beavers   Red Bank, Tenn.
    Pleasant Hunter   North Chattanooga, Tenn.
    T. B. Powell   Big Springs, Tenn. Meigs County
    Thomas Smith

46. *Names and addresses of any veterans:*
    J. M. McKenzie   Big Spring, Tenn.
    W. F. Blevins   Dayton, Tenn.
    Hiram Beavers   Red Bank, Tenn.
    Pleasant Hunter   North Chattanooga, Tenn.
    T. B. Powell   Big Springs, Tenn.
    Nute Molton   Pineland, Meigs Co., Tenn.
    Thomas Neal   Decatur, Tenn.
    Jerome King   Athens, Tenn.
    Tom Smith   Goodfield, Tenn.
    Luke King   Washington
    W. G. Allen   Dayton, Tenn.

ISAAC GRIFFITH

Born May 15, 1836, Isaac Griffith would have been 25 years old when he enlisted in Company D. His service record shows he was present at all musters and he was paroled with the regiment at the end of the war. Isaac died in 1924 and was buried in the Ramsey Cemetery in Bradley County.

His questionnaire was completed in pencil.

Most of the names given in response to Question 33 and in the attachment are members of Company D. These are exceptions: James Ed Lanis who may be James Lewis of Company C, Hanse Polk, Will Colville, Ed Carter, Jo Walker, P.L. Hairster, Jim Wills, Will Arment, Cog Russell, and Tallor [Taylor?] Russell.

GRIFFITH, ISAAC; Pvt (D) 5th (McKenzie's) Tennessee Cavalry Regiment

Residence: Cleveland, Bradley County
Enlisted: March 1, 1862 at Jacksboro by J.G.M. Montgomery for 12 months
Age: 23 on March 11, 1864 roll
Paroled: May 3, 1865 at Charlotte, North Carolina

Muster Rolls
Present	1862 Feb 14 - Apr 30	(I - 1st Regt)
Present	1862 May - Jun	(I - 1st Regt)
Present	1862 Jul - Aug	(D - 2nd Bn)
Present	1862 Sep - Oct	(D - 2nd Bn)
Present	1862 Nov - Dec	(D - 5th Regt)
Present	1863 Jan - Feb	(D - 5th Regt)
Present	1863 Mar - Apr	(D - 5th Regt)
--------	1864 Mar 11	(D - 5th Regt)
Present	1864 Nov - Dec	(D - 5th Regt)

QUESTIONNAIRE A
[1915]

1. *Name and Address:*
   Isaac Griffith, Cleveland, Bradley Co., Tennessee. RFD No. 5

2. *Current age:*
   I will bee 79 on the 15 day of May.

3. *State and county of birth:*
   I was born on Brimstone Creek, Scott co., Tennessee.

4. *State and county when enlisted:*
   I was living in Scott Co.

5. *Occupation before the war:*
   All kinds of work sutch as blacksmith and raising stock, horses, sheep, hogs and cattle.

6. *Occupation of your father:*
   Farm work and raising stock, horses, sheep, hogs and cattle.

7. *Value of property you owned:*
   We owned 375 acres of land; we owned horses, sheep, hogs, cattle. We all had lots of stock. The dollars of the stock and all kind of cattle was about eight or 9 hundred dollars. The land was worth from five to six thousand dollars. We had took away from us 7 head of horses by our neabors.

8. *Slaves owned, if any:*
   They did not own any slaves.

9. *Land your parents owned:*
   They own 375 acres of land.

10. *Value of parents' property at onset of war:*
    It worth from three to four thousand dollars.

11. *Kind of house your parents owned:*
    Two log houses two storries high. The houses stood about 20 feet apart. We used one for a kitchin and the other was our sleeping place.

12. *What kind of work you did as boy and young man:*
    When I was a boy I worked on the farm sutch as plowing, howing, and any and all kinds of work that men could do on a farm. In the winter we had lots of fun making maple sugar. We made lots of it.

13. *Kind of work your father and mother did:*
My father worked on the farm. My mother worked in the house sutch as cooking, carding, spinning, and weaving and washing. There [were] 14 in the family. She did not have any servant to help her. They cook in a fireplace. The fireplace was 7 feet wide. They did not have any stoves in them days.

14. *Servants your parents kepy, if any:*
No. They did not have any servants.

15. *Was honest toil respected in your community:*
Everybody worked and did not consider it a disgrace to do any kind of honest labor.

16. *Did white men engage in toil:*
Yes. The white men done thire own work, for their was no negro in that country at that time.

17. *Did white men idle while others worked:*
No. The men all worked and made plenty of stuff to live on.

18. *Did slave owners mingle or feel themselves better:*
They was but I herd that [those who] had slaves there wasen't any difference in them. They all seem to want to help all they could in any way. They were all on an equality.

19. *At public gatherings did slave owners mingle freely:*
No. There was not any difference. They were all friendly and kind to each other. They all tried to help their neighbor as mutch as they could.

20. *Were slave owners friendly with non-owners:*
Yes. They were all friendly and good to each other. They seem to take delight in helping each other sutch as log rollings, cornshucking and house raisings. They tried to help each other all they could and dancet [danced] all night.

21. *Did slave owners have a political advantage:*
No. It did not, for all of them tryed to do right. In the ellection time there was no buying and selling votes in them days.

22. *Were opportunities good for a poor young man:*
Yes, it was. Boys or men could make plenty of stuff for home and plenty to sell but farm products did not sell very high. A good cow could be bought for 7 dollars, corn was 33-1/3 cents bushel.

23. *Did slave owners encourage or discourage poor young men:*
They were not discouraged at all. They all help each other in any and everthing.

24. *Kind of school you attended:*
It was a primary school. We did not have any thing to study but the Old Blue Back Webster Spelling Book and some times we wrote a little. We had goose quill pens to write with.

25. *How long did you go to school:*
I went to school about one year in all, so you see I did not get to go mutch.

26. *How far was it to the nearest school:*
About a half mile to 4 miles. I have went 4 miles to school.

27. *What schools operated in your neighborhood:*
A Primary school.

28. *Was your community school public or private:*
Public school.

29. *How many months a year did it run:*
From 2 to 3 months. We had only the old blue back Webster spelling book to study.

30. *Did boys and girls attend regularly:*
Yes, as mutch as they could.

31. *Was the teacher a man or a woman:*
My school teacher was a man. We did not have any woman teachers.

32. *Year and month you enlisted:*
First day of January 1862 Jacksburrow.

33. *Your Regiment: Members of your company:*
Company D, 5th Tennessee Cavalry, Colonel McKinsey.
Captain J. G. M. Montgomery. He came to be Lutenant Colonel.
    Thos. Beagles, Captain
    Ellic [Alex] Davis, First Lieutenant
    Robbert Sloan, Sargeant
    Felix Sloan, Doctor
    Samuel Day, Doctor
    William Allen, Secand Lieutenant
    J. D. Guin, Sargent
    R. C. Lawson, Secand Sargent
    Ken Lawson
    Jake Lawson
    Nelson Lawson
    Colonel Lawson
They were all brothers, the sons of Russel Lawson.

34. *After enlistment where was your company sent:*
Kingston, Tennessee.

35. *How long before your first battle:*
It was about the last of March. We had a fight with the bushwhackers. The fight was Brimstone Creek. I lost my horse there.

36. *Your first battle:*
The first fight we had with the Yankees was at Taswell. In August we driven them back to Cumberland Gap.

37. *Your experience in the war:*
We beseiged Cumberland Gap 30 days. We drove the yanks through Kentucky where General Bragg had a 3 day fight at Peariville, Ky. He retreated back to Cumberland Gap. We, the calvery, fought here 6 days and nights in the rear of Bragg's army. On our return through the gap we campt at Taswell. At the last of October one morning the snow was about 5 inches deep. When we was getting breakfast some fool picked up a bomb shell and had it for a dog iron. It exploded and killed three men. We was ordered from there through East Tennessee into Kingston.

38. *When and where discharged:*
We received our payroll [parole] on the 3 May 1865 at Sharlet [Charlotte], N.C. We were allowed one stock and side arms.

39. *Describe your trip home:*
I came home after I got my discharge. I left Sharlet, N.C. and came through the mountains home near Cleveland, Tennessee. I came home with $2.00, two dollars and one horse and part of a suit of clothes and I had been home only 2 days when some yanky came and took my horse from me.

40. *Describe your work after the war:*
Well, the first work I done when I came home, I made bread trays and made 60 of them and sold them at one dollar a piece. I did any and all kinds of work to make a living. So, you see, I had a pretty hard time for I had nothing to commence on.

41. *A sketch of your life after the war:*
Well, I have lived in Bradley Co. since the close of the war. I have done all kinds of work. I was converted the 9 of October 1869. I joined the Missionary Baptist Church in March 1873. I have been a widower for 14 years. I was the father of 9 nine children. They are all dead but one girl. She still with me. Just her and myself is all there is of us. So I hope that this will be of help to you and I truly hope that I may live to read your history you are going to write. So I will close by saying May God who does all things will guide you in this life. And I trust we will meet where there will be no more war, where we will all be. And Amen. Isaac Griffith, Cleveland, Bradley Co., Tenn. RFD No. 5.

42. *Details of your father:*

43. *Details of your mother:*

44. *Remarks on ancestry:*

45. *Name the members of your company:*

46. *Name and address of living veterans:*

ATTACHMENT:

Isaac Griffith, Cleveland, Bradley Co., Tenn. I will be 79 years old the 15 day of May. I was borned in 1836, on Brimstone Creek, Scott Co., Tenn. I was living in Scott Co. I left home the first day of January 1862. We went to Jacksburrow to organize. Emal(?) Smith was the captain but we failed so I went to Wartburg and I fell in with Co. D, 5th Tenn Calvery so in March we went to Jacksburrow so there I enlisted in Company D of Bradley Co. Captain J. G. M. Montgomery's Company. When reorganized Montgomery became Lutenant Colonel.

    Thomas Beagles, Captain
    Ellic [Alex] Davis, First Lt.
    Robbert Sloan, Sgt
    Felix Sloan, Doctor
    Samuel Day, Doctor
    William Allen, Sekand Lt.
    J. D. Guin, Sgt.
    R. C. Lawson, Sekand Sargent
    Jake [Lawson]
    Nels [Lawson]
    Callanel [Lawson] These were brothers in Co. D
    Kin Lawson
    Hanse Polk
    James Ed Lanis
    Little Jake
    There was eleven Lawsons in my company.

I was married to Miss Winnie A. Lawson, daughter of Russel Lawson, November the 8, 1863 so I will tell you a few things about what I had when the war came up. I had two horses and a wagon, seven head of cattle, 14 head of sheep, 60 head of hogs, set of blacksmith tools, set of carpenter tools and turnin [turning] tools. A lot of household furniture, 600 bushels of corn. I lost it all.

I will tell you my part of the country where I lived in Scott County there were only 36 of disunion so we were called then the best of sitisens. We had to get out the best we could. My grandpa Griffith was an old Revolution soldier of Virginia Callvary. My pa was borned in 1774 and died in 1846. My mother died November 1859.

January 1863 we were ordered to Big Creek Gap to scout the mountains so in August we were sent on a raid in Ky. We met the eanimy at Richman and faught, our company in front. Lt. Allen commanded us. We run into their lines. We drove them, captured something over 600. From thence through East Tenn. to Dalton, Georgie. There we picketed and skirmished till the Chickamauga fight. It was the 19 of September, 1863. We fought 3 days driving them through Chattanooga.

We were ordered up in Bradley. Wheeler went on a raid through Sequatchee Valley. He got kinely tore up. Company I and A and a few of our company was left back in Bradley under Gen. Vaughn. We were in Charleston and the enemy in Calhoun. We skirmished with them. Then they made a stand at Philadelphia and we whip them. We were ordered to Dalton, Georgia the last of the war, fighting Sherman through the south to Savannie. We crost Savannie River to South Carolina, skirmishing into N.

Carolina. At Bentonville we fought Sherman 3 days. That eand the war. Wheeler commanded the left flank. On the 3 day [3rd day] was the hardest fighting I was in. We helt our line. During [the] day I shot over 300 rounds.

Late in the evening I was releaved for 4 hours. I started to our horses and came across a wounded Michigan soldier. So I built him a fire and gave him water and took one of my blankets and covered him. I forgot his name. When my time was up that I had to go back, he wanted me to write to his mother and his intended wife and tell them that he had died a honest and brave soldier and he wanted them to meet him in heaven where there would be no more parting there. When I had to leave him and go back on my duty he wanted me to shake hands with him and promise him to meet in a better world where there would be no more fighting and war. So at last I gave him my hand that I would meet him in Heaven. I had not made any profession at that time but I know he convinced me. I never got shet of that promise until I was converted so I will say that I hope and pray that we will all meet in Heaven where there will be no more wars, where all will be peace and happiness.

So I have tried to tell you some few things that I went through with, hoping they will be of enterest and help you in writing the history. So please excuse bad writing and mistakes. I hope I may live to read a true history of the old South. My daughter says to tell you to send her one of the historys for she wold love to read one. So wishing you sucksess I am ever your friend. Isaac Griffith Cleveland, Bradley Co. Tenn.

In reply to your request I will tell you some names that was in my company.

Ed Allen	Ben Grady
Jo Barksill [Barksdale]	Jim Warren
Dave McMayhan [McMahan]	John Putman
John Sutton	P. L. Hairster
John Rorse [Rose]	Jim Wills
Will Colville	Flavis Sloan
John and Ed Carter	All brothers
Joe and Tom Armes	John Willis
Joe Spears	Cred Bussel
Joe Basket	Sam Montgomery
Joe Davis	Greenbury Nelson
George Tucker	Will Arment
Jared Waid [Jarett Wade]	Cog Russel
Jo and Seth Walker	Tallor Russel
Bob Simson [Simpson]	Wash and Cal Parks
Bill Smidly [Smedley]	Dick Harris

ANDY WHITE GUFFEE

Born July 8, 1843, A. W. Guffee was 19 years old when he enlisted. He was present at all recorded musters and surrendered with the regiment at Charlotte, North Carolina.

A. W. died on 31 December 1923 and was buried beside his wife, Rebecca (25 October 1852 - 4 February 1919), in the Clark-Dry Fork Cemetery (Roane County).

His questionnaire was completed in ink and probably written by someone other than himself.

GUFFEY, A. W.; Pvt (B) 5th (McKenzie's) Tennessee Cavalry Regiment

AKA:	Guffee, A. W.; Guffie, A. W.
Residence:	Kingston, Roane County
Enlisted:	January 27, 1862 at Knoxville by J. W. Gillespie for 12 months in Kincaid's Company
Age:	20 on March 10, 1864 roll
Paroled:	May 3, 1865 at Charlotte, North Carolina

Muster Rolls

Present	1862 Jan 27 - Apr 30	(H - 1st Regt)
Present	1862 May - Jun	(H - 1st Regt)
Present	1862 Jul - Aug	(H - 2nd Bn)
Present	1862 Sep - Oct	(B - 2nd Bn)
Present	1862 Nov - Dec	(B - 5th Regt)
Present	1863 Jan - Feb	(B - 5th Regt)
Present	1863 Mar - Apr	(B - 5th Regt)
--------	1864 Mar 10 at Tunnel Hill	(Blythe's Co.)
Present	1864 Nov - Dec	(B - 5th Regt)

QUESTIONNAIRE A
February 1922

1. *Name and Address:*
   Andy White Guffee, Kingston, R. #1, Tenn.

2. *Current age:*
   79, 8 day of next July.

3. *State and county of birth:*
   Roane County, Tenn.

4. *State and county when enlisted:*
   Roane County, Tenn.

5. *Occupation before the war:*
   Farm labor.

6. *Occupation of your father:*
   Farmer.

7. *Value of property you owned:*
   Did not own any property of any kind.

8. *Slaves owned, if any:*
   No.

9. *Land your parents owned:*
   175 acres.

10. *Value of parents' property at onset of war:*
    Land, $600.00. 4 head horses value $300.00. Cattle 6 head, $90.00. $300.00 of other value.

11. *Kind of house your parents owned:*
    Hewed log house. House 1 room down 1 room overhead. Kitchen off a few feet from main house.

12. *What kind of work you did as boy and young man:*
    General farm work such as plowing, hoeing, hauling and making rails.

13. *Kind of work your father and mother did:*
    Father plowed, hoed, chopped, made rails and other farm work. Mother did cooking, weaving, spinning. Made our clothing out of cotton and flax.

14. *Servants your parents kept, if any:*
    None.

15. *Was honest toil respected in your community:*
    Yes.

16. *Did white men engage in toil:*
    Yes.

17. *Did white men idle while others worked:*
    None of this class more than 5 miles of where I lived.

18. *Did slave owners mingle or feel themselves better:*
    The men who owned slaves seemed to think themselves better than those who did not own slaves.

19. *At public gatherings did slave owners mingle freely:*
    They did not.

20. *Were slave owners and non-owners antagonistic:*
    No.

21. *Did slave owners have a political advantage:*
    No.

22. *Were opportunities good for a poor young man:*
    Not very good.

23. *Did slave owners encourage or discourage poor young men:*
    Disencouraged.

24. *Kind of school you attended:*
    Public school about 3 mo. each year.

25. *How long did you go to school:*
    About 6 mo. all told.

26. *How far was it to the nearest school:*
    2-1/2 miles.

27. *What schools operated in your neighborhood:*
    Public.

28. *Was your community school private or public:*
    Public.

29. *How many months a year did it run:*
    3 mo.

30. *Did boys and girls attend regularly:*
    Yes.

31. *Was the teacher a man or a woman:*
    Man.

32. *Year and month you enlisted:*
    Jan. 27, 1862 in Roane County at Kingston.

33. *Your Regiment: Members of your company:*
    I - 5 Tenn. commanded by G. W. McKenzie
        Lt. Jon Bly
        Bill Guffee
        J. A. Durham
        J. B. Morrison

34. *After enlistment where was your company sent:*
    Knoxville, Tenn.

35. *How long before your first battle:*
    About 7 or 8 mos.

36. *Your first battle:*
    Cumb. Gap siege to Perryville, Ky.

37. *Your experience in the war:*
    After 1st battle back to Cumb. Gap, Tenn. Scouted over East Tenn. Then under Gen. S--?-- [Col. Scott] to Richmond, when Morgan was trying to reach the prison. Thence to Parris, Ky. to destroy some bridges when we were routed by 52,000 men against 400 men.

38. *When and where discharged:*
    Apr. 26, 1865 near Shallott [Charlotte], N.C.

39. *Describe your trip home:*
    Had hard time, food and clothing.

40. *Describe your work after the war:*
    General labor, just any kind of work that I could get to do.

41. *A sketch of your life after the war:*
    Roane County. Held no office, no church relation, have had a very hard time to live.

42. *Details of your father:*
    Ephraim Guffee. [Born] Roane County, Tenn., 16 mi. south of Kingston, Tenn.

43. *Details of your mother:*
    Margaret Smith. [Daughter of] Andy Smith and [his wife] do not know. [lived in] Cumberland Co., Tenn.

44. *Remarks on ancestry:*
    Nothing further.

45. *Name the members of your company:*

46. *Name and address of living veterans:*

PLEASANT EAVES HUNTER

P. E. Hunter enlisted at the time W. W. Lillard's company was organized on July 19, 1862, and was with the regiment at its surrender.

The names given in response to Question 33 were members of Company I but a list of privates was not found.

Pleasant Eaves Hunter was born in March 1844 and died on April 26, 1928. He and his wife, Harriet B. (Whitesides) Hunter, are buried in Meigs County in the Thomas Eaves Cemetery.

HUNTER, P. E.; Cpl. (I) 5th (McKenzie's) Tennessee Cavalry Regiment

AKA:	Hunter, Pleasant E.
Residence:	Meigs County
Enlisted:	July 19, 1862 at Shiloh by W.W. Lillard for 3 years
Age:	20 on March 11, 1864 roll
Paroled:	May 3, 1865 at Charlotte, North Carolina

Muster Rolls

Present	1862 July 19 - Oct 31	(I - 2nd Bn)
Absent	1862 Nov - Dec	(I - 5th Regt)
	Absent with sick leave December 8, 1862	
Present	1863 Feb 28	(I - 5th Regt)
--------	1863 Mar - Apr	(I - 5th Regt)
	AWOL	
--------	1864 Mar 11 at Tunnel Hill	(Lillard's Co.)
Present	1864 Nov - Dec	(I - 5th Regt)

QUESTIONNAIRE A
[1922]

1. *Name and Address:*
   Pleasant E. Hunter, North Chattanooga, Box #2, Tennessee.

2. *Current age:*
   79 years old.

3. *State and county of birth:*
   State of Tennessee. Meigs County.

4. *State and county when enlisted:*
   State of Tennessee. Meigs County.

5. *Occupation before the war:*
   Farmer.

6. *Occupation of your father:*
   Farmer.

7. *Value of property you owned:*
   I was living with my father and owned no property of my own.

8. *Slaves owned, if any:*
   Neither me or my parents owned slaves.

9. *Land your parents owned:*
   My father owned about 350 acres of land.

10. *Value of parents' property at onset of war:*
    Property was valued at from $4,500 to $5,000.00.

11. *Kind of house your parents owned:*
    Log house with log kitchen, or two room house built of logs.

12. *What kind of work you did as boy and young man:*
    As a boy I worked on my father's farm. When a small boy I hoed corn, but when I grew large enough, I plowed, hoed corn, cut wheat with a cradle, and did general farm work or such work as farming required.

13. *Kind of work your father and mother did:*
    My father done farm work as I have stated above that I done, anything that was to be done on the farm. My mother did all her own house work, cooking, washing, spinning, weaving, and knitting. She spun and wove most of the material from which our clothing was made.

14. *Servants your parents kept, if any:*
    My parents kept no servants.

15. *Was honest toil respected in your community:*
    Plowing, hauling and any work that is now considered honorable was considered honorable and respectable in the community in which I lived.

16. *Did white men engage in toil:*
    All the whites in my community engaged in this kind of work as there [was] no other occupation.

17. *Did white men idle while others worked:*
    All the able bodied men in my community were industrious and I remember they were no class of men that were idle, or wasting their time.

18. *Did slave owners mingle or feel themselves better:*
    There was no class distinction in the community. All white men were considered on equal footing and as long as any man conducted himself honorable, he was looked upon as a good citizen.

19. *At public gatherings did slave owners mingle freely:*
    At the churches, schools, and public gatherings all the white population mingled on a footing of equality. There was no class distinction among the white population.

20. *Were slave owners and non-owners antagonistic:*
    There was always the best of feelings between the slaveholders and non-slaveholders, as some of the best citizens did not own slaves and some of them did own slaves.

21. *Did slave owners have a political advantage:*
    In political contests the slave question was never considered. Slaveholder and non-slaveholder would work side by side for or against an issue as their may appear [sic].

22. *Were opportunities good for a poor young man:*
    Opportunities to save and invest were encouraged in my community and it all depended upon the young man's ability to earn and save and his ability to make such investments and several young men did save, buy land and others went into business.

23. *Did slave owners encourage or discourage poor young men:*
    Any young man that was ambitious and impressed the slaveholders that he was trying to make something of himself was always encouraged and in most cases received assistance from the more prosperous men, both slaveholders and non-slaveholders.

24. *Kind of school you attended:*
    The school was a free school for the community where all white children attended, built of logs, split benches, and the Webster blue back speller was used.

25. *How long did you go to school:*
    School would run from two to three months each year. I attended school very little.

26. *How far was it to the nearest school:*
    It was about two miles to the nearest school house.

27. *What schools operated in your neighborhood:*
    There was three schools as above described in my county at that time, about 3 or 4 miles apart.

28. *Was your community school private or public:*
    The school was a public or free school.

29. *How many months a year did it run:*
    School ran from two to three months.

30. *Did boys snd girls attend regularly:*
    The boys and girls attended regular when school was in session.

31. *Was the teacher a man or a woman:*
    The teachers was most always a man.

32. *Year and month you enlisted:*
    Confederacy; June 10, 1862, Shiloh, Meigs County, Tennessee.

33. *Your Regiment: Members of your company:*
    5th Tennessee. Col. G. W. McKenzie.
    Names of members of Company "I" as follows:
          Capt. W. W. Lillard
          Lt. Jess Martin
          Lt. Jerry McKenzie
          Lt. W. F. Blevins
          Sgt's: T. H. Smith
                  Sol Crow
                  John Taff
          Corps: P. E. Hunter
                  John Todd
          Privates: Will attach roll call of Company [not found]

34. *After enlistment where was your company sent:*
    Chattanooga, Tenn.

35. *How long before your first battle:*
    Exception of a few skirmishes we were not engaged in battle until the battle of Chickamauga.

36. *Your first battle:*
    Chickamauga.

37. *Your experience in the war:*
    After battle of Chickamauga, I done picket duty 50 miles above Chattanooga on the Tennessee River, came back to Chattanooga, done picket duty until spring, then moved South to Savannah,

Ga., was engaged in battle at New Hope Church, from there to Alatoona Mtn. We were living on about half rations, was very poorly clothed, we had no tents to sleep in but layed out on the ground. I was never in prison.

From New Hope Church to Atlanta. Was engaged in battle at Atlanta, which lasted for about 2 days as I remember. Hood's army being very badly cut up, retreating to Savanah, Ga. Then crossing Savanah River to the east side, then retreating through the Carolinas to Charlotte where we [were] compelled to surrender. We were engaging in battle at Bentonville, N.C. The Federal army during this retreat destroyed all fences, cotton, other crops, buildings and etc. The Federal army was defeated at Bentonville, N.C. by Joseph E. Johnston's army. From here we went to Charlotte and surrendered and was discharged from the army and then made the march home of 13 days.

Adj. W. G. Allen of Dayton, Tennessee has written some articles on the Civil war and if you will write to him he can no doubt give you lots of valuable information. See publication of V.C. Allen on Rhea and Meigs Counties in the Confederate War.

38. *When and where discharged:*
May 12th, 1865.

39. *Describe your trip home:*
I was discharged at Charlotte, N.C. without any money. I had to march back home, leaving Charlotte Apr. 29 and arrived home May 12, 1865. I drawed ration from the Federals on my march home.

40. *Describe your work after the war:*
When I got back home the Yankees had destroyed and burned all the fences on my father's farm, so I went to work and helped my father with his farming.

41. *A sketch of your life after the war:*
I have been engaged in farming ever since I came out of the army. I have never held any office or sought any office.

42. *Details of your father:*
John Hunter. [Born] Jefferson Co., Tennessee. [Lived at] Decatur, Tennessee; my father was not in the war.

43. *Details of your mother:*
Katherine Eaves. [Daughter of] Thomas Eaves and [his wife] Don't know. [Lived at] Decatur, Tennessee.

44. *Remarks on ancestry:*
Thomas Eaves was in the Revolution War. Came to Tennessee from South Carolina, cannot say where he came from to S. Carolina. He was of Irish decent.

45. *Name the members of your company:*

46: *Name and address of living veterans:*

M. V. JONES

Martin V. Jones enlisted in the Bradley County cavalry company raised by William L. Brown at Cleveland in November 1861. On May 16, 1862 while the regiment was still the 1st (Rogers') Tennessee Cavalry Regiment that company transferred, becoming Company H of the 63rd Tennessee Infantry Regiment.

M. V. Jones (May 8, 1841 - April 30, 1938) is buried in Flint Spring Cemetery about nine miles south of Cleveland.

His questionnaire was completed in pencil.

The names given in response to Question 45 are members of Company C. Those listed in response to Question 45 are members of other units except Will Shugart who was also in Company C.

JONES, MARTIN V.; Pvt (C1) 5th (McKenzie's) Tennessee Cavalry Regiment

Also: 63rd Tennessee Infantry
Residence:
Enlisted: November 17, 1861 at Cleveland by J.W. Gillespie for 12 months in Brown's Company
Age: 20 at enlistment

Muster Rolls
Present   1861 Nov 12 - Dec 31   (C - 1st Regt)
Present   1862 Jan - Feb   (C - 1st Regt)
Present   1862 Mar - Apr   (C - 1st Regt)

JONES, M. V.; Pvt (H) 63rd (Fain's) Tennessee Infantry Regiment

Muster Rolls
--------   1862 May 1 to 16   (Brittain's Company)
--------   1862 May - Jun
            Enlisted at Charleston for 3 years by S. A. Smith
--------   1864 Apr 9   (R. A. Rutledge's Company)
            Age 25. Discharged by furnishing G. W. Cooley as substitute in 1862

QUESTIONNAIRE B
[1922]

1. *Name and address:*
   M. V. Jones, Cleveland, Bradley Co., Tenn.

2. *Age:*
   80.

3. *State and County where born:*
   Bradley, Tenn.

4. *Confederate or Federal soldier:*
   Confederate soldier.

5. *Name of your Company:*
   I, 5th Tenn.

6. *Father's occupation:*
   A Farmer.

7. *Father's name and details:*
   B. F. Jones. [*Born in*] Baltimore, Md.; [*State of*] Mareland. [*Lived*] in Vergena for several years; served as a Justice of the Peace.

8. *Mother's name and details:*
   Jane Loudderdale. [*Daughter of*] James Loudderdale, Daton [Dayton], Tenn.

9. *Remarks on ancestry:*

10. *Property owned and its value at start of war:*
    7,000 dollars.

11. *Did you or your parents own slaves:*
    5.

12. *Land owned by your parents:*
    255.

13. *Value of property owned by parents:*
    7,000 dollars.

14. *Kind of house your parents occupied:*
    A frame house.

15. *Work you did as boy and young man:*
    I worked on a farm when a boy, plow with a one horse.

16. *Work of your father and mother:*
    Cook on fire, spin on wheels to make our clothing, woved flax, made all our clouths for both male and female.

17. *Did your parents keep servants:*
    5.

18. *Was honest toil considered respectable:*
    Farming was most honorable business in the country.

19. *Did white men engage in such work:*
    They did.

20. *Were white men idle:*
    They led lives of industry.

21. *Did slave owners mingle with non-owners:*
    They did.

22. *At gatherings did slaveholders mingle:*
    They was not.

23. *Were shaveholders friendly:*
    They was.

24. *Did slaveholders have a political advantage:*
    None.

25. *Were opportunities good for poor young men:*
    Young men frequently bought farm on time.

26. *Were poor young men encouraged by slave holders:*
    They did.

27. *What kind of school did you attend:*
    Free School, one very pore.

28. *How long did you go to school:*
    About 3 years in all.

29. *How far to nearest school:*
    3 mile.

30. *What schools were in your neighborhood:*
    Man and female.

31. *Was the school private or public:*
    Publick.

32. *How many months a year did it run:*
    3 month.

33. *Did boys and girls attend regularly:*
    They did.

34. *Was the teacher a man or woman:*
    Man.

35. *When did you enlist:*
    In '61, Confederate army.

36. *Where was your Company sent first:*
    Knoxville, Tenn.

37. *How long before you were engaged in battle:*
    4 months.

38. *What was the first battle:*
    I carried dispatches.

39. *Describe your experience in the war:*
    Our diet was bread & meal that we made ourselves.

40. *When and where were you discharged:*
    I was discharged at Charlsten, Tenn.

41. *Tell something of your trip home:*
    I went home in Buggy from Charlsten.

42. *Describe your life after the war:*
    Farming.

43. *What kind of work did you do after the war:*
    Since I have ben farming, raisen stock, trading, dept. Shureff & note of Republink [notary public] for 16 years. I have rais 8 children, 6 boys and 2 girls. Have own at least 1,000 acres & divided it out with my children so I am aloan now, no fameley at all. I am not keeping hous now.

44. *Tell about some of the great men you have known:*
    I have known Andy Johnston, Landen C. Haynes, Robert Teller [Taylor], Gover Harries, James K. Polk.

45. *Names of members of your company:*

John Tucker	Martin Bates
Jim Johnston	John Bates
Capt. Britten	Col. John Roggers
James Porter	George Langston

46. *Names and addresses of any veterans:*

M. V. Jones	Cleveland, Tenn.
Bat Chambers	"
Will Cultan	"
Will Shugart	"
John Lusk	"
Henry Westmoreland	"

    M. V. Jones, Cleveland, RFD 1

LUKE M. C. KING

Luke King enlisted in McKenzie's company at the time it was organized in November 1861 and was present at every recorded muster. He surrendered with the regiment at the end of the war.

Luke M. King (1833 - 1924) and his wife, Ruthie (1838 - 1904; married 1858), are buried in the Montgomery Cemetery north of old Washington in Rhea County. Their graves are marked only with funeral home markers.

He completed both forms in 1922. Form A was completed in ink and is very hard to read; Form B was neatly written by someone other than King. The attachment to Form A, completed by W. G. Allen, is difficult to read and a few words cannot be made out.

Of the names given in response to Questions 45 and 46, only W. G. Allen and Will Godsey can be identified as members of the 5th Regiment.

KING, LUKE M.; Cpl (C5) 5th (McKenzie's) Tennessee Cavalry Regiment

Residence: Meigs County
Enlisted: November 1, 1861 at Decatur by J. W. Gillespie for 12 months in McKenzie's Company
Age: 27 at enlistment; 30 on March 11, 1864 roll
Paroled: May 3, 1865 at Charlotte, North Carolina

Muster Rolls
  Present   1862 Nov 1, 1861 - Feb 28   (B - 1st Regt)
  Present   1862 Mar - Apr   (B - 1st Regt)
  Present   1862 May - Jun   (C - 2nd Bn)
  Present   1862 Jul - Aug   (B - 2nd Bn)
  Present   1862 Sep - Oct   (C - 2nd Bn)
  Present   1862 Nov - Dec   (C - 5th Regt)
  Present   1863 Aug 31, 1862 - Feb 28   (C - 5th Regt)
  Present   1863 Mar - Apr   (C - 5th Regt)
  Present   1864 Mar 11 at Tunnel Hill   (C - 5th Regt)
  Present   1864 Dec 31   (C - 5th Regt)

QUESTIONNAIRE A

1. *Name and Address:*
   Luke M. C. King, Dayton, Tennessee, Rhea County, Rt. #1

2. *Current age:*
   89.

3. *State and county of birth:*
   Meigs County, Tennessee.

4. *State and county when enlisted:*
   Meigs County, Tenn.

5. *Occupation before the war:*
   Farming.

6. *Occupation of your father:*
   Tanner by trade.

7. *Value of property you owned:*
   No.

8. *Slaves owned, if any:*
   No.

9. *Land your parents owned:*
   120 acres.

10. *Value of parents' property at onset of war:*
    100.00.

11. *Kind of house your parents owned:*
    Log house, 2 rooms.

12. *What kind of work you did as boy and young man:*
    Plowed and hode.

13. *Kind of work your father and mother did:*
    Tanner. Cooking, spinning, and carden and weeving.

14. *Servants your parents kept, if any:*
    No.

15. *Was honest toil respected in your community:*
    Yes.

16. *Did white men engage in toil:*
    Yes.

17. *Did white men idle while others worked:*
    About one half worked.

18. *Did slave owners mingle or feel themselves better:*
    Men as did not one [own] slaves was concidered respectable as those that oned slaves.

19. *At public gatherings did slave owners mingle freely:*
    Yes. All on same footing.

20. *Were slave owners and non-owners antagonistic:*
    No.

21. *Did slave owners have a political advantage:*
    No.

22. *Were opportunities good for a poor young man:*
    Yes.

23. *Did slave owners encourage or discourage poor young men:*
    Encouraged.

24. *Kind of school you attended:*
    Some times free school and some times pay school.

25. *How long did you go to school:*
    1 year.

26. *How far was it to the nearest school:*
    1-1/2 mile.

27. *What schools operated in your neighborhood:*
    3 month free school, 3 month pay school.

28. *Was your community school private or public:*
    Public.

29. *How many months a year did it run:*
    6 month.

30. *Did boys and girls attend regularly:*
    Yes.

31. *Was the teacher a man or a woman:*
    Man.

32. *Year and month you enlisted:*
    Meigs County, Tennessee, August 25, 1861.

33. *Your Regiment: Members of your company:*
    Fifth Tennessee caverey, W. G. Allen.

34. *After enlistment where was your company sent:*
    Smiths Cross Road. Chicamagga was the first battle.

35. *How long before your first battle:*
    11 months.

36. *Your first battle:*
    Chick Magga.

37. *Your experience in the war:*
    Went to Tunel Hill. Picket out, then had one battle there and fell back to Dalton and had another battle.

38. *When and where discharged:*
    North Carolina.

39. *Describe your trip home:*
    Come home down French Broad. Rode a horse back home.

40. *Describe your work after the war:*
    Farming.

41. *A sketch of your life after the war:*
    Farming as long as could work.

42. *Details of your father:*
    Amos King. [*Born*] in Virginia; [*County*] I do not no.

43. *Details of your mother:*
    Tempa McDaniel. [*Daughter of*] Samuel McDaniel and Tempa McDaniel.

44. *Remarks on ancestry:*
    My Great grandfather was in the revolutionary war 7 years. I don't no how long my grandfather was in the war. He got wounded and was discharged.

45. *Name the members of your company:*

46. *Name and address of living veterans:*
    Luke King was parolled April 29th, 1865 at Charlotte, North Carolina, came home and went to work and made a good citizen. I have known him for 65 years.
    His old Adjt. W. G. Allen

ATTACHMENT:

Luke King, Dayton, Tenn., P.O. Washington, Rhea County, now nearing his 90 birthday, volunteered in Capt. G. W. McKenzie's company June 1861. Capt. McKenzie left Decatur, Meigs County, Tennessee July 24, 1861 with a large company, some 120. Luke King was one of that number. Their first service was at Smith's X Road (now Dayton) watching --?-- and the old Kinke [Kiuka Trace] passes across the mountain to Ky. --?-- making a company become Co. C of 5th Tenn. cavalry.

They were in the battles of Fishing Creek, Murfreesboro, Chickamauga and made the first raid around Rosecrans' army. Helped destroy Rosecrans' waggons at Dunlap in Sequachee Valley. At Farmington, Tenn. the regiment lost 70 men in a hand to hand fight. Luke King was in all the battles fought on W. and A. RR in Johnston's retreat to Atlanta and under Hood to Jonesboro. Then in Wheeler's raid through North Georgia and Tennessee in Alabama and then with Wheeler around Dalton to North Alabama.

And when Gen. Corse drove Gen. Wheeler from North Alabama the 5th Tenn. was at Collinsville and was the last regiment to reach the Coosa River. We had to swim the horses across and when driven in they would float downstream so that they would not make the landing where they could climb the river bank. Wheeler rode up and said, "Adjutant, detail a good swimmer. Let him mount a good horse and tie 4 or 5 to the tail of the one that was being ridden." I detailed Luke King for I knew he had been raised on the river.

He swum the river 38 times in that chilly November morning by my orders. Swum the horse he was riding and, turning the horse over for a detail of men to take care of and swum to north side, take charge of another set that was ready to be led over. Some Georgia Col. rode up and gave King $100 bill to swim his mule over, making 39 times King swum Emery(?) River that cold November morning in 1864.

Furnished by W. G. Allen, Dayton, Tenn.

QUESTIONNAIRE B
[1922]

1. *Name and address:*
   L. M. King, Dayton R #1, Tennessee.

2. *Age:*
   89 years.

3. *State and County where born:*
   Meigs Co., Tennessee.

4. *Confederate or Federal soldier:*
   Confederate.

5. *Name of your Company:*
   Co. C, 5th Tennessee.

6. *Father's occupation:*
   Tanner.

7. *Father's name and details:*
   Amos King. [*Born in*] Virginia. [*Lived in*] Meigs Co., Tennessee.

8. *Mother's name and details:*
   Temp McDaniel. [*Daughter of*] Sam McDaniel and [*his wife*] don't know.

9. *Remarks on ancestry:*
   My Great Grandfather served 7 yrs in Rev. War. Grandfather McDaniel served 5 yrs in Rev. War, was wounded and discharged.

10. *Property owned and its value at start of war:*
    1 horse.

11. *Did you or your parents own slaves:*
    None.

12. *Land owned by your parents:*
    100 acres.

13. *Value of property owned by parents:*
    100 acres land, 1 horse and tools to farm with 1 horse.

14. *Kind of house your parents occupied:*
    Log house, 2 rooms.

15. *Work you did as boy or young man:*
    Farmed, plowed, hoed and made one horse crop myself.

16. *Work of your father and mother:*
    Father did the work at the Ten Yard. Mother did the cooking, spinning, weaving and making garments.

17. *Did your parents keep servants:*
    None.

18. *Was honest toil considered respectable:*
    Yes.

19. *Did white men engage in such work:*
    Yes.

20. *Were white men idle:*
    None.

21. *Did slave owners mingle with non-owners:*
    Yes. They even worked with their slaves.

22. *At gatherings did slaveholders mingle:*
    Yes.

23. *Were slaveholders friendl;y or antagonistic:*
    Slave holders and non-slave holders were friendly.

24. *Did slaveholders have a political advantage:*
    Yes.

25. *Were opportunities good for poor young men:*
    Yes.

26. *Were poor young men encouraged by slave holders:*
    Encouraged.

27. *What kind of school did you attend:*
    Free school.

28. *How long did you go to school:*
    About 12 mo.

29. *How far to nearest school:*
    1-1/2 miles.

30. *What schools were in your neighborhood:*
    Free schools & Pay schools.

31. *Was the school private or public:*
    Public.

32. *How many months a year did it run:*
    About 6 mo.

33. *Did boys and girls attend regularly:*
    Yes.

34. *Was the teacher a man or woman:*
    Man.

35. *When did you enlist:*
    Meigs Co., Tenn., July 22, 1861.

36. *Where was your Company sent first:*
    Smith Cross Road.

37. *How long before you were engaged in battle:*
    Scouting.

38. *What was the first battle:*
    Big Creek Gap.

39. *Describe your experience in the war:*
    Left Meigs Co., went to Smith Cross Roads. Scout Mt. to Kingston, captured some renigades. From Kingston to Jacksboro; scouted Mt. to Ky., Cumberland Gap. Picketing & scouting until the Perryville & Cumberland Gap fight. Fought for 20 days. Left there and went to Tenn. Chickamauga. Discharged at Raleigh, N.C.

40. *When and where were you discharged:*
    Raleigh, N.C.

41. *Tell something of your trip home:*
    Stacked arms at Griffith, N.C. Rode horse back home.

42. *Describe your life after the war:*
    Farming.

43. *What kind of work did you do after the war:*
    Farmed since war, until too old. Lived in Tenn. Baptist church.

44. *Tell about some of the great men you have known:*

45. *Names of members of your company:*
    | Co C: | W. P. Thomison | Dayton, R. 1, Tenn. |
    | | H. L. W. Furguson | Spring City, Tenn. |
    | | Tip Harris | " " |
    | | Ephr. Garraway | Dayton, Tenn. |
    | | G. W. Brewer | " |
    | | J. L. Henry | " |
    | | Asa Johnson | " |

46. *Names and addresses of any veterans:*
    | | W. G. Allen | Dayton, Tenn. |
    | | Will Godsey | " |
    | | W. M. Melton | " |
    | | Joseph Henry | " |

JEREMIAH M. McKENZIE

Jeremiah McKenzie, nephew of the regimental commander, Col. G. W. McKenzie, was born December 21, 1830, according to Questionnaire B. He died April 28, 1922, and the questionnaire was completed by a family member after his death. His headstone in the McKenzie Cemetery in Meigs County has the birth date as December 22, 1831.

The questions and responses were typewritten on legal size sheets and the form itself was not returned.

McKENZIE, J.; 2Lt (I) 5th (McKenzie's) Tennessee Cavalry Regiment

AKA:	McKenzie, Jeremiah; McKinzie, Jeremiah
Residence:	Decatur, Meigs County
Enlisted:	July 19, 1862 at Shiloh by W. W. Lillard for 3 years
Age:	32 on March 11, 1864 roll; 33 on POW roll

Muster Rolls

Present	1862 Jul 19 - Oct 31	(I - 2nd Bn)
Present	1862 Nov - Dec	(I - 5th Regt)
Present	1863 Feb 28	(I - 5th Regt)
Present	1863 Mar - Apr	(I - 5th Regt)
--------	1864 Mar 11 at Tunnel Hill	(Lillard's Co.)
Absent	1864 Nov - Dec	(I - 5th Regt)

Captured August 19, 1864 in Meigs County

POW   1864 Aug 19
        Captured at Decatur
       1865 May 13
        Released on oath at Johnson's Island, Ohio

QUESTIONNAIRE B
November 16, 1922

1. *Name and address:*
   Jeremiah M. McKenzie, Big Spring, Tennessee.

2. *Age:*
   Ninety one years of age since December 21st, 1921.

3. *State and County where born:*
   State of Tennessee, Meigs County.

4. *Confederate or Federal soldier:*
   Confederate in Civil War. American soldier in Mexican War.

5. *Name of your Company:*
   Company "I", 5th Tennessee Calvary.

6. *Father's name:*
   Benjamin Franklin McKenzie.

7. *Father's name and details:*
   Farmer. Born near Big Springs, Meigs County, Tenn. Lived there till his death. He served his county as County Judge or Chairman, Justice of the Peace and Tax Assessor.

8. *Mother's name and details:*
   Nancy Casey and she was the daughter of William and Elizabeth Casey. She lived near Big Springs, Meigs County, Tennessee.

9. *Remarks on ancestry:*
   The subject of this sketch is of Scotch Irish descent. All of his ancestors having imigrated to America from Scotland, some of them coming over during Colonial times and the great grand father of J.M. McKenzie having fought in the battle of Yorktown in the Revolutionary War. Col. George W. McKenzie who commanded the Fifth Tennessee Regiment, known as the "Fighting Fifth," was an uncle.

10. *Property owned and its value at start of war:*
    Owned the farm of 600 acres upon which the subject of this sketch lived and died, having died April 28th, 1922.

11. *Did you or your parents own slaves:*
    Father owned twelve slaves.

12. *Land owned by parents:*
    Six hundred acres, which subject of sketch inherited.

13. *Value of property owned by parents:*
    Fifteen hundred dollars, or more.

14. *Kind of house your parents occupied:*
    Old style ten room Colonial home.

15. *Work you did as boy and young man:*
    From the time large enough did light work on the farm. At the age of fifteen years ran away from home and went to war with Mexico.

16. *Work of your father and mother:*
    He was a farmer and tobacco raiser and mother weaved, spun flax, and did the ordinary work of housewives of that day with servants.

17. *Did your parents keep servants:*
    Had twelve slaves and used part of them in the home as servants. Three, two women and one man.

18. *Was honest toil considered respectable:*
    Yes.

19. *Did white men engage in such work:*
    They acted more as over-seers.

20. *Were white men idle:*
    Comparatively few.

21. *Did slave owners mingle with non-owners:*
    While they were in separate and distinct classes, yet the Southern gentleman owning slaves always recognized worth and merit under all circumstances, and mingled freely with those who were respectable and honorable regardless of prosperity.

22. *At gatherings did slaveholders mingle:*
    As a rule they did.

23. *Were slaveholders friendly to non slaveholders:*
    Yes. A friendly feeling existed until about the time of the breaking out of the war, at which time it became tense.

24. *Did slaveholders have a political advantage:*
    Until the question became one of live topic and abolition agitated, it did not.

25. *Were opportunities good for poor young men:*
    Yes.

26. *Were poor young men encouraged by slave holders:*
    Encouraged.

27. *What kind of school did you attend:*
Common free schools.

28. *How long did you go to school:*
Only attended the fall session of three months each year up to the age of fifteen.

29. *How far to nearest school:*
Two miles.

30. *What schools were in your neighborhood:*
Common schools only.

31. *Was the school private or public:*
Public only.

32. *How many months a year did it run:*
Three.

33. *Did boys and girls attend regularly:*
Yes.

34. *Was the teacher a man or woman:*
Man.

35. *When did you enlist:*
When but a lad of fifteen years, ran away from home and enlisted in Captain Lillard's Company and went to Mexico. Was under the command of General Scott and fought in the various battles until the capture of the city of Mexico and Santa Anna. On the 19th day of July 1862 volunteered and joined Company "I" commanded by Captain W. W. Lillard and was mustered into service on that date at old Shilo Church, Meigs County, Tennessee. Was commissioned a second lieutenant and soon thereafter first lieutenant of said company, being cavalry.

36. *Where was your Company sent first:*
To Chattanooga, Tenn., where it was attached to General Bragg, who was organizing the Army of Tennessee for Kentucky Campaign. This Company remained in Chattanooga only a few days and was ordered to Sparta, Tennessee and attached to Comb's Battalion. [37]

On the advance of General Bragg this Company "I" was detached and ordered to report to General Bragg and acted as his escort on his advance into Kentucky. But when the fact was made known to General Bragg that Company "I" had enlisted with the intention of being attached to the fighting Fifth Tennessee Cavalry, a regiment commanded by Col. G. W. McKenzie, General Bragg ordered Captain Lillard to report to Colonel McKenzie which he did at once and Company "I" became a part of the fighting Fifth Tennessee Cavalry and from thence forth the illustrious record made by the fighting Fifth Cavalry is the history of Company "I," for this Company was with the Fifth Tennessee in all the battles and skirmishes from Perryville, Ky. to Greensboro, N.C., and was one Company that Col. McKenzie said so often could be depended upon at all times.

The subject of this sketch in 1864 when the Fifth Tennessee left Athens, Ga. with Wheeler's Command was detailed with others to go under Adjutant Allen to tear up a railroad, cut telegraph wires, which was done, and then they moved on up the old East Tennessee, Virginia and Georgia Railroad and intercepted their command and, upon arriving in the neighborhood of their home, Company "I" were allowed to go home and see their families and at a certain time thereafter rejoin their commands. While at home visiting his family he was captured by a Yankee home guard, who had never seen service and they were properly nick-named "Hog Back Company."

He was sent to Johnson's Island, Ohio to a Yankee prison where he suffered many privations and while there ate the hind leg of a dog that had been cooked and presented to him by a comrad who had caught this canine wandering around in prison following a Yankee officer, choked him to death, cleaned and cooked him.

At the age of ninety one at the old homestead in Meigs County on the 28th day of April 1922 he died and was laid to rest with his kindred and fathers in the McKenzie burial grounds. The subject of this sketch married Margaret Masoner a short time before the Civil war. She was the daughter of Isaac Masoner, one of the wealthiest planters in Meigs County, who owned over one hundred slaves at the beginning of the war. To this union was born and who still survive, five children as follows:

    G. A. McKenzie, a farmer of Meigs County.
    B. G. McKenzie, Attorney General of the 18th Judicial Circuit of Tennessee, who resides in Dayton.
    L. T. McKenzie, an Attorney at Law who also resides at Dayton
    Dr. J. R. McKenzie, of Cleveland, Tenn., who is a physician and Surgeon, and
    Mrs. Nancy Jane Hale, of Welch, Oklahoma.

                                      This is correct. B. G. McKenzie
                                      Dayton, Tenn. Nov. 16, 1922

37. *How long before you were engaged in battle:*

38. *What was the first battle:*

39. *Describe your experience in the war:*

40. *When and where were you discharged:*

41. *Tell something of your trip home:*

42. *Describe your life after the war:*

43. *What kind of work did you do after the war:*

44. *Tell about some of the great men you have known:*

45. *Names of members of your company:*

46. *Names and addresses of any veterans:*

EBENEZER MELVIN PATTEN MOORE

From the service record below, it appears that E. M. P. Moore enlisted as a volunteer in McLin's company in October 1861 but was discharged for disability in August 1862 and forced back into service by conscription early in 1863.

The questionnaire, completed by his daughter, is neatly written.

MOORE, E. M. P.; Pvt (H) 5th (McKenzie's) Tennessee Cavalry Regiment

Residence: Washington County
Enlisted: October 21, 1861 at Knoxville by J. W. Gillespie for 12 months in McLin's Company
Age: 28 at enlistment; 29 on certificate

<u>Muster Rolls</u>

Absent	1861 Oct 21 - Dec 31	(G - 1st Regt)
	At home on sick furlough	
Present	1862 Jan - Feb	(G - 1st Regt)
Present	1862 Mar - Apr	(G - 1st Regt)
Absent	1862 May - Jun	(Mullendore's Co.)
	At home sick	
--------	1862 Jul - Aug	(G - 2nd Bn)
	Discharged August 20, 1862 by order of Gen. Smith	
--------	1862 Sep - Oct	(H - 2nd Bn)
	Discharged August 20, 1862	
--------	1862 Dec 31	(H - 5th Regt)
	Discharged September 9, 1862	
Present	1863 Jan - Feb	(H - 5th Regt)
	Transferred from camp of instruction by Col. Blake January 7, 1862	
Absent	1863 Mar - Apr	(H - 5th Regt)
	At home sick since March 7, 1863	
--------	1864 Mar 11 at Tunnel Hill	(Mullendore's Co.)
	On Post duty	

1862 Aug 12
Certificate of Disability: Typhoid fever settled in bowels and lungs, signed Samuel Day
1864 Feb 9
At Bristol, assigned duty in commissary department

QUESTIONNAIRE B

1. *Name and address:*
   Ebenezer Melvin Patten Moore, Bristol, Tenn.

2. *Age:*

3. *State and County where born:*
   Washington County, Tenn.

4. *Confederate or Federal soldier:*
   Confederate.

5. *Name of your company:*
   Fifth Tennessee Calvary commanded by Col. G. W. McKenzie, Pegram's brigade, Hunt's Division[?], Army of the Cumberland [Army of Tennessee]

6. *Father's occupation:*
   Farmer.

7. *Father's name and details:*
   James Moore. [*Born in*] Rockbridge County, Va., near Natural Bridge, Va. After his mother's death he lived with his grandfather, R. W. Samuel Benson (near Lexington Va.). At the age of 20 yrs he came to Washington County, Tenn. and married.

8. *Mother's name and details:*
   Miss Sarah Collom. [*Daughter of*] Jonathan Collom & Martha Serch. [*Lived*] Near Philadelphia, Tenn. and settled at Washington College, Tenn.

9. *Remarks on ancestry:*
   Jonathan Collom was among the first elders in Salen Church at Washington College, the first Presbyterian Church in this part of the country. Daniel Moore, the paternal grandfather of E. M. P. Moore was a mason and his family came from Ireland, being closely related to the Moores who were the principal characters in the little historical narrative "The Captives of Abi Valley."

10. *Property owned and its value at start of war:*
    Small farm.

11. *Did you or your parens own slaves:*
    No.

12. *Land owned by your parents:*

13. *Value of property owned by parents:*

14. *Kind of house your parents occupied:*
    Six room log house.

15. *Work you did as boy and young man:*
    E. M. P. Moore's father died while he was a small boy and he supported two sisters by working on the farm and between seasons clerking in a store.

16. *Work of your father and mother:*
    All kinds of farm and domestic work.

17. *Did your parents keep servants:*
    None.

18. *Was honest toil considered respectable:*
    Such work was considered honorable by these sturdy farmers, most of whom came into Tennessee wilderness from Virginia, to clear lands and establish homes.

19. *Did white men engage in such work:*
    Yes.

20. *Were white men idle:*
    Energetic white people.

21. *Did slave owners mingle with non-owners:*
    No decided difference in a social way in my county.

22. *At gatherings did slaveholders mingle:*
    Yes.

23. *Were slaveholders friendly or antagonistic:*
    Friendly.

24. *Did slaveholders have a political advantage:*
    No.

25. *Were opportunities good for poor young men:*
    E. M. P. Moore, a student at Washington College, expected to be a physician, but the death of his father and the war made this impossible.

26. *Were poor young men encouraged by slave holders:*
    They were not discouraged.

27. *What kind of school did you attend:*
    Washington College, formerly Martin's Academy.

28. *How long did you go to school:*

29. *How far to nearest school:*
    Two miles.

30. *What schools were in your neighborhood:*

31. *Was the school private or public:*

32. *How many months a year did it run:*

33. *Did boys and girls attend regularly:*
    Yes.

34. *Was the teacher a man or woman:*

35. *When did you enlist:*
    June, 1861.

36. *Where was your Company sent first:*
    On guard at Swan Pond, having been sent there from Knoxville to guard the East Tenn, Va. and Georgia Ry.

37. *How long before you were engaged in battle:*

38. *What was the first battle:*
    Fought at Zollicoffer, Tazewell, Tenn., Cumberland Gap & Fishing Creek.

39. *Describe your experience in the war:*
    Was present the night the bridges at Strawberry Plains and Zollicoffer burned. After that, detailed to the comissary dept. and ordered to report to Capt. John M. Orr. After this he [Moore] held the position of purchasing agent until the war closed. A severe attack of typhoid unfitted him for further active service as a soldier. Lack of proper food and exposure also caused the disease to leave him in a weakened condition.

40. *When and where were you discharged:*

41. *Tell something of your trip home:*

42. *Describe your life after the war:*
    Farming & school teaching and church work.

43. *What kind of work did you do after the war:*
    After the war E. M. P. Moore married Susan Cowan King of Holston Valley, Sullivan County, Tenn. where he resided as a farmer, tax collector and school teacher for many years, later moving to Bristol, Tenn. and making his home with his daughter, Mrs. Doak Moore Delaney.

44. *Tell about some of the great men you have known:*

45. *Names of members of your company:*
    John Benson (deceased)

46. *Names and addresses of any veterans:*
    Mahlon Cowan, Bristol, RFD, Tenn.

JOHN F. SEHON

Born December 27, 1845, John Sehon was only 16 years old when he enlisted in March 1862. Although he was not discharged as under age when the regiment was reorganized under the conscript act in May 1862, he was discharged for that reason one year later. He mentions later service in Cocke County with Texas Rangers but no record of that service has been found.

The questionnaire was neatly written in ink.

The names given in response to Question 45 were members of Company F except that "Broxies" cannot be identified.

SEAHON, JOHN F.; Pvt (F) 5th (McKenzie's) Tennessee Cavalry Regiment

AKA: Seehon, John F.
Residence: Grainger County
Enlisted: March 13, 1862 at Knoxville by A. L. Mims for 12 months
Age: 17 on March 12, 1864 roll; 17 on certificate

<u>Muster Rolls</u>

Present	1862 Jan - Feb (dated Apr 30, 1862)	(E - 1st Regt)
Absent	1862 Feb 28 - Jun 30	(E - 2nd Bn)

On sick furlough from June 15, 1862 by Col. McLin

--------	1862 Jul - Aug	(F - 2nd Bn)

Detailed as courier to Col. Ben Allston August 12, 1862 by order of Col. McLin

Absent	1862 Sep - Oct	(F - 2nd Bn)

Left without permission at Rose's Furnace September 20, 1862

Present	1862 Nov - Dec	(F - 5th Regt)

AWOL from September 10 to November 11, 1862

Absent	1863 August 31, 1862 - Feb 28	(F - 5th Regt)

AWOL 86 days

--------	1863 Mar - Apr	(F - 5th Regt)
--------	1864 Mar 12 at Tunnel Hill	(F - 5th Regt)

Discharged

1863 May 17
Certificate of discharge at Boston, Ky. Underage
1863 Jun 4
Included on register of discharges

QUESTIONNAIRE B
April 24, 1922

1. *Name and address:*
   John F. Sehon, Monterey, Tenn.

2. *Age:*
   77 the 27 day of December 1922.

3. *State and County where born:*
   Tenn., Cocke County.

4. *Confederate or Federal soldier:*
   Confederate, you bet.

5. *Name of your Company:*
   Co. F, 5th Tenn. Cav.

6. *Father's occupation:*
   Farmer and smith.

7. *Father's name and details:*
   W. G. Sehon. [*Born in*] Overton County, Tenn. [*Lived at*] Morristown, East Tenn. He voted for the Union but finally went with his State.

8. *Mother's name and details:*
   Barthana Clark. [*Daughter of*] James Clark and E. Danniels. [*Lived*] on Holston River, Grainger County, now Hamblin County.

9. *Remarks on ancestry:*

10. *Property owned and its value at start of war:*

11. *Did you or your parents own slaves:*
    1 fine negro man, fine smith, and my father refused 25 hundred dollars for him, and 1 negro woman, mother of five children.

12. *Land owned by your parents:*
    209 acres.

13. *Value of property owned by parents:*
    I suppose negroes and all about $25 thousand.

14. *Kind of house your parents occupied:*
    Log house ceiled and weather boarded. If I remember 8 rooms and 2 porches.

15. *Work you did as boy and young man:*
Happy to say I farmed in summer and went to school in fall at Morristown, E. Tenn. Worked through crops with negroes. Soon as I could split middles I went to plowing, used the hoe also when necessary. I was raised to work. My father often told me he was going to learn me to work and if after grown if I didnt have to work I could let alone awful easy.

16. *Work of your father and mother:*
All this was carried on, flax raised and hackeled and spun on little wheel. My mother seen after it, worked herself and worked the negro woman.

17. *Did your parents keep servants:*
7 as originally stated.

18. *Was honest toil considered respectable:*
As well as I remember we had awful good neighbors who respected seemingly honest toil.

19. *Did white men engage in such work:*
Yes, with few exceptions.

20. *Were white men idle:*
Very few.

21. *Did slave owners think themselves better:*
I think not. Mostly social and kind, as well I remember.

22. *At gatherings did slaveholders mingle:*
Seemed they did.

23. *Were slaveholders friendly or antagonistic:*
Seemed kind and friendly and visited each other.

24. *Did slaveholders have a political advantage:*
I can't remember any difference.

25. *Were opportunities good for poor young men:*
Seemed chances were favorable.

26. *Were poor young men encouraged by slave holders:*
Not to my knowledge.

27. *What kind of school did you attend:*
Academy at Morristown.

28. *How long did you go to school:*
Can't remember, so in broken doses.

29. *How far to nearest school:*
3/4 mile.

30. *What schools were in your neighborhood:*
Free schools partly.

31. *Was the school private or public:*
Public.

32. *How many months a year did it run:*
About 3 months.

33. *Did boys and girls attend regularly:*
They seemed to, as well as I remember.

34. *Was the teacher a man or woman:*
Men mostly, now and then a woman.

35. *When did you enlist:*
I joined the 17 day of Mch. 1862 at Clinton, Tennessee.

36. *Where was your Company sent first:*
To Kentucky, if not mistaken. Not positive, they kept us on the scout most all the time.

37. *How long before you were engaged in battle:*
Don't remember.

38. *What was the first battle:*
Brimstone, Scott County, Tenn.

39. *Describe your experiences in the war:*

40. *When and where were you discharged:*
Camp Pine Knot, Ky. I got my discharge burned up in J. H. Ray's dwelling, my cousin in the county of Overton.

41. *Tell something of your trip home:*

42. *Describe your life after the war:*
I left E. Tenn., came to Overton Co. Went into goods business with 2 of my cousins, J. H. Ray and his Bro. in law Hampton.

43. *What kind of work did you do after the war:*
Mercantile while in Overton. Livery business at this place and been J.P. for about 18 years. 6 yrs. in Overton and near 12 yrs in Putnam County. I have belonged to Methodist Church about 50 years. Have tried to live right and honestly with my fellow man.

44. *Tell about some of the great men you have known:*

45. *Names of members of your company:*
G. W. McKenzie was Colonel of 5th Tenn. Cav. and
>A. L. Mimms was our Capt.
>G. W. Harper, 1st Lt.
>R. A. McNabb, 2d Lt.   Henries,
>Dervett [Dewitt], 3d Lt.   Williams,
>Lewis was sargent   Broxies,
>and the Stoklies   McMahans,
>and the Lewises   Hopkinses,
>Jas. Allen   Headricks,
>G. W. Carter   Evanses.

Most all the company was from Cocke County, East Tennessee. I will say we had brave good boys in the Co. Got accustomed to Bushwhackers.

I got strain with Government wagon, lifting stalled wagon. I never have got over, never will. My Captain asked if I didnt want to go home. I told him I had got used to the army and wasent caring. I knew I wasent able hardly for duty. He said I had been faithful and if I would promise one thing he would fix for me to go home. I asked him what it was. He said it was to come back to his company. I told him if I ever joined any company I would. I wasent able for the army and did left for McMinn Co.

So much fighting above Knoxville back and forth to Bristol. I went to Cocke County with some Texas Rangers and was no good for service so I was advised to retire and wound my way horseback to McMinn. Stayed with an Uncle by name of Jno. Sharp and Bro. in Law Morelock. Hope [helped?] them all I could working. I hope I have complied with your request as far as able. Anything I can do, use me. I am most truly yours, John F. Sehon

46. *Names and addresses of any veterans:*
>Uncle Sherd Horn   Monterey, Tenn.
>Revt. G. D. Byrns
>Jno. H. Lea   Livingston, Tenn.
>D. A. Bagwell   Monterey, Tenn.
>Henry Paregon   Livingston, Tenn.
>F. M. Copeland   Monterey, Tenn.
>J. R. Copeland
>Captan, father in law [?]
>Dec Nett, Carrier, Tenn. [?]

I will add here they kept our command in the mountains most all the time, Tenn. and Ky. Cumberland Mtns. I was on detail as courier under Col. Austin [Allston] near Cumberland Gap when we had the enemy beseiged in the Gap. Palmer was in command of the enemy, if I remember correctly. Later on 2 companies of our command was cut off at Boston, Ky. and we took the mountains and was 4 days without rations, little corn.

WILLIAM MANING WHITSON

William Whitson enlisted in March 1863 and was captured seven months later in the fierce fighting at Farmington (Shelbyville) during Wheeler's first Tennessee raid just after the battle of Chickamauga. He spent the next seventeen months in prison, being exchanged in early 1865.

The questionnaire was neatly written in pencil.

Of the names given in response to Question 45, Ben Wood, Bob Hopkins, and Joseph Hopkins cannot be identified as members of the 5th Regiment.

WHITSON, WILLIAM; Pvt (F) 5th (McKenzie's) Tennessee Cavalry Regiment

Residence:
Enlisted: March 15, 1863 at Newport by A. L. Mims for the war
Age: 18 on March 12, 1864 roll

Muster Rolls
Present   1863 Mar - Apr   (F - 5th Regt)
--------   1864 Mar 12 at Tunnel Hill   (F - 5th Regt)
              Prisoner

POW   1863 Oct 7
              Captured at Shelbyville
            1865 Mar 15
              Paroled at Camp Morton, Indiana and forwarded to Point Lookout, Maryland for exchange

QUESTIONNAIRE B

1. *Name and address:*
   William Maning Whitson, Cocke Co.

2. *Age:*
   Eighty years.

3. *State and County where born:*
   Cocke Co., Tennessee.

4. *Confederate or Federal soldier:*
   Confederate.

5. *Name of your Company:*
   F, 5th Tennessee Caverey.

6. *Father's occupation:*
   Blacksmith.

7. *Father's name and details:*
   William Maning Whitson. [*Born*] Cocke Co., Tenn.

8. *Mother's name and details:*
   Miss Didy McMahan. [*Daughter of*] Eli McMahan. [*Lived at*] Cosby's Creek, Cocke Co., Tennessee.

9. *Remarks on ancestry:*

10. *Property owned and its value at start of war:*
    A small mountain farm.

11. *Did your parents own slaves:*
    No.

12. *Land owned by your parents:*
    A small piece.

13. *Value of property owned by parents:*

14. *Kind of house your parents occupied:*
    One room log house.

15. *Work you did as boy and young man:*
    Worked twenty-five years. Plowed and hoed.

16. *Work of your father and mother:*
    Blacksmithing. Housework, cooking, spinning, weaving.

17. *Did your parents keep servants:*
    No.

18. *Was honest toil considered respectable:*
    Yes.

19. *Did white men engage in such work:*
    They did.

20. *Were white men idle:*
    None.

21. *Did slave owners mingle with non-owners:*
    Yes. They associated together, mixed and mingled with each other.

22. *At gatherings did slaveholders mingle:*
    Yes.

23. *Were slaveholders friendly or antagonistic:*
    They were friendly with each other.

24. *Did slaveholders have a political advantage:*
    Yes, they helped.

25. *Were opportunities good for poor young men:*
    Yes.

26. *Were poor young men encouraged by slave holders:*
    They were encouraged by the slave holder.

27. *What kind of school did you attend:*
    Very poor schools.

28. *How long did you go to school:*
    About two years.

29. *How far to nearst school:*
    2 miles.

30. *What schools were in your neighborhood:*
    Small primary schools.

31. *Was the school private or public:*
    Publick.

32. *How many months a year did it run:*
    3 months.

33. *Did boys and girls attend regularly:*
    Very little.

34. *Was the teacher a man or woman:*
    Man.

35. *When did you enlist:*
    1862 Oct. at Knoxville, Tenn.

36. *Where was your Company sent first:*
    Big Creek Gap, Cumberlin Mountain.

37. *How long before you were engaged in battle:*
    4 months.

38. *What was the first battle:*
    London, Kentucky.

39. *Describe your experience in the war:*
    We were ordered back to Tenn., then to Chickamoga Battle. Lived hard in camp, hungry and cold in prison 18 months.

40. *When and where were you discharged:*
    Richmond, Va.

41. *Tell something of your trip home:*
    Walked home, wore out, hungry, and very bad clothed.

42. *Describe your life after the war:*
    Clearing, making rails, plowing, hoeing.

43. *What kind of work did you do after the war:*
    Farming. I have lived in Cocke Co., Tenn.

44. *Tell about some of the great men you have known:*

45. *Names of members of your company:*
    Ben Wood   Ely Whitson
    Jasper Hopkins   Steve Whitson
    Bob Hopkins   James Whitson
    Joseph Hopkins

46. *Names and addresses of any veterans:*
    James Wood, Newport, Tenn.
    Ben Wood, Excelsior Springs, Mo.
    E. B. Cotes, Newport, Tenn.
    Joe Morell, Newport, Tenn.

JOHN WOLFE

Born May 11, 1845, John Wolf was 17 years old when he enlisted December 1862. His service record is somewhat inaccurate in showing he was AWOL as a final entry, as he indicated in response to Question 38, he was with one of the companies separated from Wheeler in East Tennessee in the August 1864 raid on Sherman's supply line.

The questionnaire responses are neatly written in ink.

All of the names listed in response to Question 33 were members of Company G except that Perry Cantwell cannot be so identified.

WOLF, JOHN, JR.; Pvt (G) 5th (McKenzie's) Tennessee Cavalry Regiment

Residence:
Enlisted: December 17, 1862 at Sneedville by Capt. Graham for 3 years
Age:

Muster Rolls
Present	1862 Nov - Dec	(G - 5th Regt)
Absent	1863 Jan - Feb	(G - 5th Regt)
	AWOL from February 11, 1863	
Present	1863 Mar - Apr	(G - 5th Regt)
	AWOL 36 days	
--------	1864 Mar 12 at Tunnel Hill	(G - 5th Regt)
	AWOL	

QUESTIONNAIRE A
February 27, 1922

1. *Name and address:*
   John Wolfe, Luther, Tenn.

2. *Current age:*
   77, be 78 the 11th of May 1922.

3. *State and county of birth:*
   Hancock Co., Tenn.

4. *State and county when enlisted:*
   Hancock Co., Tenn.

5. *Occupation before the war:*
   Farmer.

6. *Occupation of your father:*
   Farmer.

7. *Value of property you owned:*
   I did not own anything. I was just 17 turned into 18. My father died when I was 8 years old.

8. *Slaves owned, if any:*
   My father owned 1 slave.

9. *Land your parents owned:*
   Something like a hundred acres.

10. *Value of parents' property at onset of war:*
    We owned some stock, I don't remember.

11. *Kind of house your parents owned:*
    A log house with kitchen to cook and eat in.

12. *What kind of work you did as boy and young man:*
    Plow and hoe. Cut wheat and all kinds of farm work done in those days.

13. *Kind of work your father and mother did:*
    My father worked all kinds of work on the farm. My mother carded wool and cotton and spun it into yarn and made it into cloth. Knit sox and stockings and spun flax and made it into cloth that made our clothes. She done her own weaving cloth.

14. *Servants your parents kept, if any:*
    Did not keep any servants all the time. When needed help, would hire as many as needed.

15. *Was honest toil respected in your community.*
    It was.

16. *Did white men engage in toil:*
    They did.

17. *Did white men idle while others worked:*
The most of them worked. I knew of 2 that did not work very much.

18. *Did slave owners mingle with non slave owners:*
They did as far as I remember.

19. *At public gatherings did slave owners mingle freely:*
I think they did.

20. *Were slave owners and non-owners antagonistic:*
They was all friendly.

21. *Did slave owners have a political advantage:*
I don't remember.

22. *Were opportunities good for a poor young man:*
I think they was. If he had any chance at all.

23. *Did slave owners encourage or discourage poor young men:*
They were not discouraged.

24. *Kind of school you attended:*
Free school.

25. *How long did you go to school:*
About 4 months.

26. *How far was it to the nearest school:*
1/2 mile.

27. *What schools operated in your neighborhood:*
Free school and I remember one subscription school.

28. *Was your community school private or public:*
Public.

29. *How many months a year did it run:*
2 or three.

30. *Did boys and girls attend regularly:*
Not much.

31. *Was the teacher a man or a woman:*
1 man and 1 woman.

32. *Year and month you enlisted:*
I don't remember the exact date but it was in the fall '61, I think Oct.

33. *Your Regiment: Members of your Company:*
5th Tennessee Cavelary

David Wilder	Shade Wilder	James Debusk	Perry Cantwell
James Wilder	Chas. Wilder	Joe Debusk	Thomas Cantwell
Thomas Wilder	Wiley Wilder	John Cantwell	David Cantwell

Nick Wolf	Wiley McCoy	Elbert Day	Jessie Day
Harmon Hayse	Ad Peaters	Etsal Arnett	Col. McKenzie
Jeff Lamb	Silvester Walker	Guss Arnett	Lt. Col. Montgomery
Kale Bell	Peet Walker	James Gully	Capt. John Graham
Bill Gibson	Greenfield Taylor	Alf Hale	
	Harve Tarter	C. D. Spence	

34. *After enlistment where was your company sent:*
Kentucky.

35. *How long before your first battle:*
Don't remember.

36. *Your first battle:*
At Richmond, Ky. We used small arms and Artilry and we drove them back.

37. *Your experience in the war:*
Went to Big Creek Gap, Tenn. In battle at Louden, Tenn. I was at Chicamauga, Tenn. Fought battle at Tunel Hill, Ga., New Hope Church, Ga., Atlanta, Ga., Wagons Burrow [Waynesboro], Ga., Ring Gole [Ringgold], Ga., Duck River, Tenn. You wanted to know how I fared. I liked to starved part of the time, slept on the ground, mud and snow. My clothes was very thin most of the time. I had measles but did not go to hospital. Had my feet to feeeze in stirrups many times.

38. *When and where discharged:*
Spring '65. Was not discharged. Got cut off from my command on raid that Wheeler made and surrendered at Cumblin [Cumberland] Gap, Ky.

39. *Describe your trip home:*
I walked home which was 40 miles. I went this trip after night.

40. *Describe your work after the war:*
I went to Va. and worked on a farm. After that went to the old Blue Grass Section and hired to a Rebel soldier and, after I left him, came back to Tennessee and married.

41. *A sketch of your life after the war:*
Bin farmer the most of my life while I was able to work. I have lived most all of my life in Hancock Co. I have lived in the Baptist Church for 35 or more years.

42. *Details of your father:*
George Wolfe. [*Born at*] Treadway, Hancock Co., Tenn. [*Lived at*] Flat Gap near Treadway, Tenn.

43. *Details of your mother:*
Luisa Miligan. [*Daughter of*] Sollomon Miligan. I don't know her [*mother's*] name. She was a Morgan. [*Lived*] on War Creek near Luther, Tenn.

44. *Remarks on ancestry:*
My mother's people come from Ireland. My father sounded to be Duch [Dutch].

45. *Name the members of your company:*

46. *Name and address of living veterans:*

TOLIVER WOOD

Toliver Wood first enlisted in the 26th Tennessee Infantry Regiment but was discharged as under age. In February 1863 he enlisted in Company F, 5th Regiment, probably as a conscript. Listed as AWOL on the March 12, 1864 muster and on Federal rolls as a deserter in December 1863, he was probably one of the many rebel soldiers who deserted from Bragg's army at Dalton in the winter of 1863 - 64.

The questionnaire was completed in pencil and is very dim.

Of the names given in response to Questions 45 and 46, none appears on muster rolls of the 5th Regiment.

WOOD, TOLIVER; Pvt (C) 26th Tennessee Infantry Regiment

Enlisted: June 27, 1861 at Camp Cumming by Gen. Gillespie in Capt. Edwin Allen's Company

Muster Rolls
Present	1861 to Dec 31	(C - 26th Regt)
Present	1862 to Feb 28	(C - 26th Regt)
Present	1862 to Apr 30	(C - 26th Regt)
Absent	1862 Oct 27, 1861 - Jun 30	(C - 26th Regt)

    Left with baggage train

----- --- -- [undated roll]
    On list of men detained as train guards

-------- 1864 Jan 22 at Dalton (Capt. George Stewart's Co.)
    Discharged on account of being of non-conscript age at the expiration of his term of service. Age 18.

WOOD, TOLLIVER; Pvt (F) 5th (McKenzie's) Tennessee Cavalry Regiment

AKA: Woods, Tolliver
Residence: Cocke County
Enlisted: February 20, 1863 at Newport by Capt. Mims for 3 years
Age: 18 on March 12, 1864 roll

Muster Rolls
-------- 1863 Aug 31, 1862 - Feb 28   (F - 5th Regt)
    Detailed at Knoxville by Dr. Morton, date not known

Present 1863 Mar - Apr   (F - 5th Regt)

-------- 1864 Mar 12 at Tunnel Hill   (F - 5th Regt)
    Absent without permission

POW 1863 Dec 16
    Released on oath at Knoxville as rebel deserter

QUESTIONNAIRE B
[1922]

1. *Name and address:*
   Toliver Wood, Excelsior Springs, Missouri.

2. *Age:*
   76 yrs. 8 mo. 5 days.

3. *State and County where born:*
   Tennessee, Cocke County.

4. *Confederate or Federal soldier:*
   Confederate.

5. *Name of your Company:*
   Capt. Allen's (Co. C), 26th Tenn. Inf.

6. *Father's occupation:*
   Farmer.

7. *Father's name and details:*
   Gipson Wood. [*Born*] Newport, Cocke Co., Tennessee. He spent his entire life in this place.

8. *Mother's name and details:*
   Polly Sisk. [*Daughter of*] Tolliver Sisk and Nancy Kelly. [*Lived at*] Newport, Tennessee.

9. *Remarks on ancestry:*

10. *Property owned and its value at start of war:*

11. *Did you or your parents own slaves:*
    Yes, three.

12. *Land owned by your parents:*
    About 300 acres.

13. *Value of property owned by parents:*
    About $4,200.

14. *Kind of house your parents occupied:*
    A four room house. Three rooms were frame building, the other one was built of hewn logs.

15. *Work you did as boy and young man:*
    I worked on the farm and did all the different kinds of farm work such as plowing, hoeing, grubbing, making rails, building fences, clearing woodlands.

16. *Work of your father and mother:*
    General farming. My mother's duties were all the different household work such as cooking, sewing, spinning, weaving, laundry work and drying fruit, knitting. Also they raised, colored and spun all their cotton for clothing.

17. *Did your parents keep servants:*
    Yes, five (5).

18. *Was honest toil considered respectable:*
    Yes, all sort of honest work was considered respectable and honorable.

19. *Did white men engage in such work:*
    Yes. Most all of them did this kind of work.

20. *Were white men idle:*
    Idle men were very few and they did not employ any one to do their work.

21. *Did slave owners mingle with non-owners:*
    The men who owned slaves mingled freely and always associated with the men who did not.

22. *At gatherings did slaveholders mingle:*
    Yes. They mingled on a footing of equality.

23. *Were slaveholders friendly or antagonistic:*
    Very friendly.

24. *Did slaveholders have a political advantage:*
    No.

25. *Were opportunities good for poor young men:*
    The opportunities for such were not good.

26. *Were poor young men encouraged by slave holders:*
    Encouraged.

27. *What kind of school did you attend:*
    Subscription schools for several years, then free schools.

28. *How long did you go to school:*
    A short term each year for eight years.

29. *How far to nearest school:*
    About 1-1/2 miles.

30. *What schools were in your neighborhood:*
    Just one public school.

31. *Was the school private or public:*
    Public.

32. *How many months a year did it run:*
    Very seldom had more than 4 months term.

33. *Did boys and girls attend regularly:*
    Yes.

34. *Was the teacher a man or woman:*
    A man all the time excepting 1 term.

35. *When did you enlist:*
    I enlisted in the service of the Confederate Government at my residence in the month of June 1861.

36. *Where was your Company sent first:*
    Entered into service in Knoxville, Tenn. Company was sent to Jamestown.

37. *How long before you were engaged in battle:*
    In the early spring of 1862.

38. *What was the first battle:*
    Fort Donaldson battle. Our regiment was captured with the exception of disabled and wagoners.

39. *Describe your experience in the war:*
    We went to Nashville, Tenn. From there to Murphysboro, Tenn. And there we gave over what we had over to the government lot. They took us to Knoxville. There I served as train guard for six months.

40. *When and where were you discharged:*
    At Knoxville, Tenn. after I had served 18 months in the infantry.

41. *Tell something of your trip home:*
    I went home on the train and stayed at home about two months.

42. *Describe your life after the war:*
    I joined Capt. Mim's Co. F, 5th Tenn Cavalry, Col. McKenzie's Regt.

43. *What kind of work did you do after the war:*
    I lived in Tenn. and farmed the 6 years after the war closed. Then I came to Ray Co., Missouri in the spring of 1871 and have spent these 51 years on my farm here with the exception of two years I spent in Tenn. during this time. I was under Gen. Palmer's command and was stationed at Big Creek Gap at the foot of the Cumberland Mt. near Jacksborough. I scouted the mountains for about ten months from Big Creek Gap to Cumberland Gap and from there to the Chicamauga fight.

44. *Tell about some of the great men you have known:*

45. *Names of members of your company:*
Lewis Allen	David Hartsell	Francis Griffen
Austin Hickey	John Hickey	Alex Gray

46. *Names and addresses of any veterans:*
    Billy Ringo, Richmond, Mo.
    Reeves Gant, Lawson, Mo.
    Joe Duvall, Richmond, Mo.
    Huston Shelton, Excelsion Springs, Mo.

WILLIAM JEFFERSON WOODY

Jefferson Woody enlisted in Thomas Gorman's company when it was organized in November 1861. His company was one of those separated in East Tennessee from Wheeler's command during the August 1864 raid. Consequently he was not with the regiment when it surrendered.

The responses to the questionnaire were neatly written in ink, probably by someone other than the veteran.

Of the names listed in response to Question 45, only Gum Hopkins cannot be identified as a member of Company F, 5th Regiment.

WOODY, JEFFERSON; Pvt (F) 5th (McKenzie's) Tennessee Cavalry Regiment

Residence: Cocke County
Enlisted: November 22, 1861 at Knoxville by J. W. Gillespie for 12 months in Gorman's Company
Age: 21 at enlistment; 20 on March 12, 1864 roll

Muster Rolls

Present	1862 Jan - Feb	(E - 1st Regt)
Present	1862 Feb 28 - Jun 30	(E - 2nd Bn)
--------	1862 Jul - Aug	(F - 2nd Bn)
	Detailed as courier to Col. Ben Allston by order of Col. McKenzie Aug. 12, 1862	
Present	1862 Sep - Oct	(F - 2nd Bn)
Absent	1862 Nov - Dec	(F - 5th Regt)
	AWOL since November 19, 1862	
Present	1863 Aug 31, 1862 - Feb 28	(F - 5th Regt)
	Absent 47 days	
Present	1863 Mar - Apt	(F - 5th Regt)
Present	1864 Mar 12 at Tunnel Hill	(F - 5th Regt)

QUESTIONNAIRE B
[1922]

1. *Name and address:*
   William Jefferson Woody, Dandridge, Rte. 6, Tennessee.

2. *Age:*
   82 years, 6 mo. 27 days.

3. *State and County where born:*
   Burke Co., N. Carolina.

4. *Confederate or Federal soldier:*
   Confederate.

5. *Name of your Company:*
   F Co. Cavalry, 5th Tennessee. Known as McKinsley's Reg.

6. *Father's occupation:*
   Farming and gold mining.

7. *Father's name and details:*
   William Tate Woody. [*Born at*] Marion, McDowell Co., N. Carolina within 6 mi. of Marion and was not in the war.

8. *Mother's name and details:*
   Valencia Branch. [*Daughter of*] Stephen Branch [*and*] Tabitha Carson Branch. [*Lived in*] Burke Co.

9. *Remarks on ancestry:*

10. *Property owned and its value at start of war:*
    I entered the war when 20 years old and had not acquired anything but personal property except a horse.

11. *Did you or your parents own slaves:*
    No.

12. *Land owned by your parents:*

13. *Value of property owned by parents:*

14. *Kind of house your parents owned:*
    A log house with two rooms.

15. *Work you did as boy and young man:*
 I worked on the farm as plow boy for 2 years and also worked in gold mine. Some rich white men did not work in the field but poor ones did.

16. *Work of your father and mother:*
 My father worked in gold mine and farmed, providing our meager fare for Mother to cook on the fire. We always had a patch of cotton from which Mother spun and wove our clothes.

17. *Did your parents keep servants:*
 No.

18. *Was honest toil considered respectable:*
 Work of this sort was considered respectable and honorable.

19. *Did white men engage in such work:*
 Yes.

20. *Were white men idle:*
 A few men, not many, were able to hire their work done.

21. *Did slave owners mingle with non-owners:*
 The men that I knew did not feel themselves any better than those who did not own slaves. They mingled freely.

22. *At gatherings did slaveholders mingle:*
 Yes.

23. *Were slaveholders friendly or antagonistic:*
 A friendly feeling.

24. *Did slaveholders have a political advantage:*
 Not then. I think the poor man had equal chance with the rich.

25. *Were opportunities good for poor young men:*
 Opportunities were scarce even for a hard worker.

26. *Were poor young men encouraged by slave holders:*
 In most instances they were encouraged.

27. *What kind of school did you attend:*
 Free school in a little log cabin.

28. *How long did you go to school:*
 About 9 mo. I attended 3 schools for 3 mo. as a term.

29. *How far to nearest school:*
 A mile.

30. *What schools were in your neighborhood:*

31. *Was the school private or public:*
Public.

32. *How many months a year did it run:*
Three months.

33. *Did boys and girls attend regularly:*
Yes, the house was always full.

34. *Was the teacher a man or woman:*
The first two were men and the third was a woman.

35. *When did you enlist:*
At Newport, Tenn., Cocke Co. I enlisted in the service in the month of Sept. 1862.

36. *Where was your Company sent first:*
To Knoxville.

37. *How long before you were engaged in battle:*

38. *What was the first battle:*
The first battles were so numerous we called them scrimages [skirmishes] and the first was Chuckey Knob.

39. *Describe your experience in the war:*
I was in the battle of Chickamauga which lasted 3 days. The Yankees fell back into Chattanooga on Sunday evening after we had fought 3 days. At times we had plenty to eat and at others we went hungry. We had to take the weather mostly as it came, exposed to all sorts of things. We were kept mostly in the Cumberland Mts. among the bushwhackers.

40. *When and where were you discharged:*
The Confederate soldiers were not discharged. The officers told us we could go home, it was over.

41. *Tell something of your trip home:*
I was close to home when Lee surrendered and was so glad to turn my face toward home that I do not remember anything in particular that happened on the way.

42. *Describe your life after the war:*
Farming.

43. *What kind of work did you do after the war:*
Since being out of arms I have farmed some and been a miller some. Have lived in Cocke and Jefferson Counties, Tenn ever since the war. I am a member of the Missionary Baptist Church. I have made an honest living tho have worked hard for it, never being able to get any com-

pensation from the Government in any way or from the State. I have made application for State Aid at different times but have never been successful in getting any help from that source. If you could have any influence with the Board I would appreciate your helping me.

44. *Tell about some of the great men you have known:*
I was associated some with Bob Taylor. I believe our Captain Mims was a great man.

45. *Names of members of your company:*
   Capt. Lem Mims, Newport, Tenn.
   Russell McNabb, Newport, Tenn.

Alex DeWitt	Toliver Woods
William Bryant	Jim Allen
Will Denton	Will Allen
George Harper	Dave Stokely
William Harper	Will Stokely
Ben Hopkins	Elisha Stokely
Gum Hopkins	Jim Huff
Baxter Hopkins	George Brooks
Jasper Hopkins	John Bolen [Bowling]
George Carter	Summerfield Hedrick
Grundy Lewis	Marshall Henry

   All of Newport, Tennessee

46. *Names and addresses of any veterans:*
   Col. A. R. Swann, Dandridge, Tenn.
   Joseph Rutherford, Dandridge, Tenn.
   J. P. Graves, Morristown, Tenn
   James Welch, Newport, Tenn.
   Dave Stokely, Newport, Tenn.
   J. R. Knisley, Newport, Tenn.
   George McClannahan, Newport, Tenn.
   John Lovell, Bybee, Tenn.
   Bill Strange, Rankin, Tenn.
   Vincent Fine, Rankin, Tenn.

NOTES

1. William B. Sloan (unpublished diary) is more specific in stating that his brother Robert was injured "in the early months of 1863" by a runaway horse, that Allen afterward was acting adjutant until the Battle of Chickamauga when Robert returned to duty as adjutant and served until December of that year when he was transferred to Macon, Georgia.

2. It was not until March 24, 1864, that Col. McKenzie issued an order appointing Lt. Allen to the position of adjutant.

3. Current research has not uncovered evidence of Allen's promotion to the rank of major. J. L. Blackwell served as major from January 7, 1862, until his resignation December 1, 1863. In a special order dated December 16, 1863, at Cave Springs, Capt. Mims was appointed acting major.

4. Brimstone Creek rises in Scott County, Tennessee. On February 3, 1862, Lt. Col. White reported to Col. Leadbetter from Morgan County that "a portion of our regiment engaged the enemy yesterday." On March 28, 1862, Col. Leadbetter at Knoxville ordered Vaughn's 3rd Tennessee Infantry and a squadron of cavalry from Kingston into Morgan and Scott Counties where they met and skirmished with the enemy. (*Official Records*, I - 7, 119)

5. His service record states that Lt. William F. Horner, Company G, was discharged for reasons of disability on March 5, 1863. Isaac N. Horner, Bugler of Company G, died from an accidental gunshot wound near Williamsburg on April 20, 1863. No other Horners are listed in regimental records.

6. Gen. John Pegram's raid was March 22 to April 1, 1863.

7. In the *Confederate Veteran*, Volume 21 (October 1913), p. 488, A. C. Terhune of Danville, Kentucky, recorded details of Col. Pegram's raid.

8. Federal Gen. George W. Morgan evacuated Cumberland Gap September 17, 1862, and was pursued into Kentucky by Confederate forces.

9. This raid into Eastern Kentucky took place July 25 to August 6, 1863, and is recorded in *Official Records* as "Scott's Raid." (I-20, Part 2, pp. 828-843). Its purpose was to gather cattle and horses and to divert Federal troops from John H. Morgan who had started on July 2 into Kentucky, Indiana, and Ohio.

10. See Note 5 above.

11. His service record shows that Allen was furloughed.

12. In other versions of this event, John Loyd was not along. Allen appears to have this episode confused with his retreat from the Chickamauga battlefield where he was wounded and stated that John Loyd accompanied him.

13. William Sloan's diary entry for August 17, 1863 and succeeding days gives details of this foray to Murphy. His version is different, not only as to date but in other important ways.

14. The Sander's Raid into East Tennessee took place June 14 to 24, 1863, preceding Scott's Raid referenced above.

15. On September 2, 1863, William Sloan was advance vidette at Loudon. His report of events at Loudon is different from Allen's.

16. Lt. M. D. Lansford was captured at Irvine, Kentucky, on July 21, 1863, and in prison until June 11, 1865, and could not have been with the regiment at this time.

17. William Sloan, who was also wounded at Chickamauga, wrote on September 19, 1863, that Capt. Reagan and Adjt. Allen "each have flesh wounds which are not serious." On September 20 he wrote that the three of them "passed through Ringgold and took up lodging for the night." On the 21st they separated, each making his way to the home of friends to recuperate. Sloan did not mention that John Loyd was present.

18. His service record states that John Loyd was captured in Murry County, Georgia, about February 15, 1864, and died at Rock Island Barracks, Illinois, of chronic bronchitis. Grave #993.

19. See J. T. Crawford's questionnaire.

20. Allen is sometimes very specific about dates but at other times vague.

21. His service record states that Lt. William Guffee was killed in battle near Tunnel Hill on February 5, 1864.

22. See Note 3 regarding Allen's promotion.

23. His service record states that William Deatherage was wounded and left near Dalton on August 15, 1864.

24. His service record states Asberry Talley as wounded and left near Dalton August 15, 1864.

25. See Note 16.

26. In his questionnaire, Isaac Griffith stated that Companies A and I and a few of Company D were detached and remained in East Tennessee under Gen. John C. Vaughn, but no other records have been found to confirm this.

27. See the questionnaire of Jeremiah McKenzie.

28. Dr. William T. Delaney was regimental surgeon of the 8th Tennessee Cavalry.

29. Gen. Felix Robertson returned to East Tennessee with Gens. Dibrell and Williams and participated in the Saltville Battle. His account of moving through North Carolina and Georgia to rejoin Wheeler is given in the *Confederate Veteran*, Volume 30 (September 1922), p. 334.

30 V. C. Allen enlisted April 5, 1862, in the 1st (Rogers') Tennessee Cavalry Regiment, predecessor organization of the 5th Regiment. He was discharged on July 8, 1862, for disability and later joined the 3rd Tennessee Infantry Regiment.

31 See Allen's attachment to L. M. King's questionnaire.

32 Identified in current records as Hamilton's Tennessee Cavalry Battalion.

33 Muster Rolls for Company D do not include John or J. D. Rains.

34 There was also a company of girls in Clarksville, Tennessee.

35 An unsigned company report dated October 31, 1862, stated, "This company was first at Battle Creek when the Federals vacated that place; then marched to Sparta, Tennessee." Maj. Lewis' Battalion has not been identified. See the response of J. M. McKenzie, Question 35.

36 The Tennessee Centennial Commission publications list Maj. S. H. Colms as commander of the 1st (Colms') Tennessee Infantry Battalion (also called the 20th Tennessee Infantry Battalion) but it has not been possible to establish that this unit accompanied Gen. Braxton Bragg on his Kentucky Campaign. No references have yet been found for a Col. Combs.

37 See Note 36.

FORM A

The chief purpose of the following questions is to bring out facts that will be of service in writing a true history of the Old South. Such a history has not yet been written. By answering these questions you will make a valuable contribution to the history of your State.

In case the space following any question is not sufficient for your answer, you may write your answer on a separate piece of paper. But when this is done, be sure to put the number of the question on the paper on which the answer is written, and number the paper on which you write your answer.

Read all the questions before you answer any of them. After answering the questions given, if you desire to make additional statements, I would be glad for you to add just as much as you desire.

1. State your full name and present Post Office address:

2. State your age now:

3. In what State and County were you born?

4. In what State and County were you living when you enlisted in the service of the Confederacy, or of the Federal Government?

5. What was your occupation before the war?

6. What was the occupation of your father?

7. If you owned land or other property at the opening of the war, state what kind of property you owned, and state the value of your property as near as you can:

8. Did you or your parents own slaves? If so, how many?

9. If your parents owned land, state about how many acres:

10. State as near as you can the value of all the property owned by your parents, including land, when the war opened:

11. What kind of house did your parents occupy? State whether it was a log house or frame house or built of other materials, and state the number of rooms it had:

12. As a boy and young man, state what kind of work you did. If you worked on a farm, state to what extent you plowed, worked with a hoe, and did other kinds of similar work:

13. State clearly what kind of work your father did, and what the duties of your mother were. State all the kinds of work done in the house as well as you can remember — that is cooking, spinning, weaving, etc.:

14. Did your parents keep any servants? If so, how many?

15. How was honest toil — as plowing, hauling and other sorts of honest work of this class — regarded in your community? Was such work considered respectable and honorable?

16. Did the white men in your community generally engage in such work?

17. To what extent were there white men in your community leading lives of idleness and having others do their work for them?

18. Did the men who owned slaves mingle freely with those who did not own slaves, or did slave-holders in any way show by their actions that they felt themselves better than respectable, honorable men who did not own slaves?

19. At the churches, at the schools, at public gatherings in general, did slaveholders and non-slaveholders mingle on a footing of equality?

20. Was there a friendly feeling between slaveholders and non-slaveholders in your community, or were they antagonistic to each other?

21. In a political contest in which one candidate owned slaves and the other did not, did the fact that one candidate owned slaves help him in winning the contest?

22. Were the opportunities good in your community for a young man — honest and industrious — to save up enough to buy a small farm or go into business for himself?

23. Were poor, honest, industrious young men, who were ambitious to make something of themselves, encouraged or discouraged by slave-holders?

24. What kind of school or schools did you attend?

25. About how long did you go to school altogether?

26. How far was it to the nearest school?

27. What school or schools were in operation in your neighborhood?

28. Was the school in your community public or private?

29. About how many months in the year did it run?

30. Did the boys and girls in your community attend school pretty regularly?

31. Was the teacher of the school you attended a man or a woman?

32. In what year and month and at what place did you enlist in the Confederate or of the Federal Government?

33. State the name of the regiment, and state the names of as many members of your company as you remember:

34. After enlistment, where was your campany sent first?

35. How long after your enlistment before your company engaged in battle?

36. What was the first battle you engaged in?

37. State in your own way your experiences in the war from this time on until the close. State where you went after the first battle — what you did, what other battles you engaged in, how long they lasted, what the results were; state how you lived in camp, how you were clothed, how you slept, what you had to eat, how you were exposed to cold, hunger and disease. If you were in the hospital or in prison, state your experience here:

38. When and where were you discharged?

39. Tell something of your trip home:

40. What kind of work did you take up when you came back home?

41. Give a sketch of your life since the close of the Civil War. stating what kind of business you have engaged in, where you have lived, your church relations, etc. If you have held an office or offices, state what it was. You may state here any other facts connected with your life and experience which has not been brought out by the questions.

42. Give the full name of your father: -----; born ----- at -----; in the county of -----; state of -----. He lived at -----. Give also any particulars concerning him, as official position, war services, etc.; books written by, etc.

43. Maiden name in full of your mother: -----; She was the daughter of ----- and his wife ----- who lived at -----.

44. Remarks on ancestry. Give here any and all facts possible in reference to your parents, grand-parents, great-grandparents, etc., not included in the foregoing, as where they lived, office held, Revolution or war services; what country the family came from to America; where first settled, county and state; always giving full names (if possible) and never referring to an ancestor simply as such without giving the name. It is desirable to include every fact possible and to that end the full and exact record from old Bibles should be appended on separate sheets of this size, thus preserving the facts from loss:

45. Give the names of all the members of your Company you can remember: (If you know where the Roster is to be had, please make special note of this.)

46. Give here the NAME and POST OFFICE ADDRESS of living veterans of the Civil War, whether members of your company or not.

FORM B

In case the space following any question is not sufficient for your answer, you may write your answer on a separate piece of paper. But when this is done, be sure to put the number of the question on the paper on which the answer is written, and number the paper on which you write your answer.

Read all the questions before you answer any of them. After answering the questions given, if you desire to make additional statements, I would be glad for you to add just as much as you desire.

1. State your full name and present post office address:

2. State your age now:

3. In what State and County were you born?

4. Were you a Confederate or Federal Soldier?

5. Name of your Company?

6. What was the occupation of your farher?

7. Give full name of your father -----; born at -----; in the County of -----; State of -----; He lived at -----. Give also any particulars concerning him, as official position, war services, etc.; books written by him, etc.

8. Maiden name in full of your mother -----; she was the daughter of ----- and his wife ----- who lived at -----.

9. Remarks on ancestry. Give here any and all facts possible in reference to your parents, grand-parents, great-grandparents, etc., not included in the foregoing as where they lived, offices held, Revolutionary or other war service; what country they came from to America; first settled ---- county and State; always give full names (if possible) and never referring to an ancestor as such without giving the name. It is desirable to include every fact possible, and to that end the full and exact record from old Bibles should be appended on separate sheets of this size, thus preserving the facts from loss.

10. If you owned land or other property at the beginning of the war, state what kind of property you owned, and state the value of your property as near as you can:

11. Did you or your parents own slaves? If so, how many?

12. If your parents owned land, state about how many acres:

13. State as near as you can the value of all the property owned by your parents, including land, when the war opened:

14. What kind of house did your parents occupy? State whether it was a log house or frame house or built of other material, and state the number of rooms it had:

15. As a boy and young man, state what kind of work you did. If you worked on a farm, state to what extent you plowed, worked with a hoe and did other kinds of similar work. (Certain historians claim that white men would not do work of this sort before the war.)

16. State clearly what kind of work your father did, and what the duties of your mother were. State all the kinds of work done in the house as well as you can remember — that is, cooking, spinning, weaving, etc.

17. Did your parents keep any servants? If So, how many?

18. How was honest toil — as plowing, hauling and other sorts of honest work of this class — regarded in your community? Was such work considered respectable and honorable.

19. Did the white men in your community generally engage in such work?

20. To what extent were there white men in your community leading lives of idleness and having others do their work for them?

21. Did the men who owned slaves mingle freely with those who did not own slaves, or did slaveholders in any way show by their actions that they felt themselves better than respectable, honorable men who did not own slaves?

22. At the churches, at the schools, at public gatherings in general, did slaveholders and non-slaveholders mingle on a footing of equality?

23. Was there a friendly feeling between slaveholders and non-slaveholders in your community, or were they antagonistic to each other?

24. In a political contest, in which one candidate owned slaves and the other did not, did the fact that one candidate owned slaves help him any in winning the contest?

25. Were the opportunities good in your community for a poor young man, honest and industrious, to save up enough to buy a small farm or go in business for himself?

26. Were poor, honest, industrious young men, who were ambitious to make somethimg of themselves, encouraged or discouraged by slaveholders?

27. What kind of school or schools did you attend?

28. About how long did you go to school altogether?

29. How far was it to the nearest school?

30. What school or schools were in operation in your neighborhood?

31. Was the school in your community private or public?

32. About how many months in the year did it run?

33. Did the boys and girls in your community attend school pretty regularly?

34. Was the teacher of the school you attended a man or woman?

35. In what year and month and at what place did you enlist in the service of the Confederacy or of the Federal Government?

36. After enlistment, where was your Company sent first?

37. How long after enlistment before your Company engaged in battle?

38. What was the first battle you engaged in?

39. State in your own way your experience in the War from this time on to its close. State where you went after the first battle — what you did and what other battles you engaged in, how long they lasted, what the results were; state how you lived in camp, how you were clothed, how you slept, what you had to eat, how you were exposed to cold, hunger, and disease. If you were in the hospital or prison, state your experience there.

40. When and where were you discharged?

41. Tell something of your trip home.

42. Give a sketch of your life since the close of the Civil War, stating what kind of business you have engaged in, where you have lived, your church relations, etc. If you have held any office or offices, state what it was. You may state here any other facts connected with your life and experience which has not been brought out by the questions.

43. What kind of work did you take up when you came back home?

44. On a separate sheet, give the names of some of the great men you have known or met in your time, and tell some of the circumstances of the meeting or incidents in their lives. Also add any further personal reminiscence. (Use all the space you want.)

45. Give the names of all the members of your Company you can remember. (If you know where the Roster is to be had, please make special note of this.)

46. Give the NAME and POST OFFICE ADDRESS of any living Veterans of the Civil War, whether members of your Company or not; whether Tennesseans or from other States.

INDEX

1st (Carter's) Tennessee Cavalry Regiment 56
1st (Colm's) Tennessee Infantry Battalion 131
1st (Rogers') Tennessee Cavalry Regiment 1,86, 131
1st Louisiana Tigers 7
1st Louisiana (Scott's) 8,11
1st Tennessee Cavalry 15,44
2nd East Tennessee (Col. Coon)
2nd Regiment 1
2nd Tennessee (Ashby's) 7,11,20
2nd Tennessee Cavalry 11,15,24
2nd Tennessee Federal Regiment 50
3rd Tennessee Infantry Regiment 131
3rd Tennessee Volunteers 2
3rd (Brazelton's) Tennessee Cavalry Battalion 56
3rd Tennessee (Vaughn's) 24
4th Cavalry (Anderson's) 23
4th Tennessee 50
5th Ohio Regiment 9
5th Regiment 1,6,46,61
5th Tennessee 61,131
5th Tennessee (McKenzie's) 8,10,13,15,20,34,50, 64,70,77,107,112,116,120
5th Tennessee Cavalry 6,11,15,18,45,47,62,68, 75,81,86,113
6th Georgia (Hart's) 8,11
8th Illinois Battery 12,16
8th Tennessee Cavalry 130
8th Texas 18,20
9th Tennessee Battalion 15,20,23,50
9th Tennessee Cavalry 20
11th Texas 20
16th Tennessee Battalion 8
18th Battalion 26
19th Tennessee Infantry 18
20th Tennessee Infantry Battalion 131
26th Infantry 46
26th Tennessee 18,47,49
26th Tennessee Infantry Regiment 51,120,121
43rd Regiment 6
43rd Tennessee Infantry 29
54th Virginia (Coal's) 16
63rd Tennessee (Fain's) Infantry Regiment 86

- A -

ABINGTON, VA 24
ABLE, Perry 30
ADAIRSVILLE, GA 19
ADAMS, Betsey 52 Nancy 53; Sam 53
AKIN, Maj. 15,23
ALABAMA 68,69; see also— Collinsville, Decatur, Gadsden, Jackson County, Larkinsville
ALATOONA 19
ALATOONA MOUNTAIN 85
ALLEN, Adjt. 69,102,130; Adj. W.G. 85; Ann Frazier 5; Barbara F. 30; Capt. 121; Capt. Edwin 120; Ed 76; G.W. 30; George W. 2,24; Jas. 111; Jim 128; Judge V.C. 5; Lewis 123; Lt. 129; T.A. 24,30; V.C. 6,24,30,85,131; Valentine 5,30; W.G. 27, 30,46,51,69,90,93,97; Will 128; William 73,75; William Gibbs 1 - 30; Willie 14
ALLEN'S Alabama Brigade 6,19, Company 120
ALLSTON, Col. 8,111; Col. Ben 107,124
ALLSTON'S 1st Louisiana 8
ALTAMONT, TN 23
ANDERSON, Col. Paul 23
ARMENT, Will 70,76
ARMES, Joe 76; Tom 76
ARMY OF TENNESSEE 20
ARNETT, Etsal 119; Guss 119
ASHBY, Col. 9; Col. H.M. 11,15
ASHBY'S, Brigade 15,19; 2nd Tennessee 7,8,9, 11,20; Tennessee Brigade 6
ASHVILLE, NC 27,50,65,69
ATCHLEY, John 22
ATHENS, GA 102
ATHENS, TN 21,69
ATLANTA, GA 20,21,34,44,45,50,65,68,85,94, 119
ATLANTA & MACON RAILROAD 20
AUGUSTA, GA. 21,25,26

- B -

BAGWELL, D.A. 111
BAIRD, Gen. 17
BAIRD'S BRIGADE 12
BALTIMORE, MD 87
BARBERVILLE, KY 7
BARBOURSVILLE, KY 9
BARKSILL [BARKSDALE], Jo
BASKET, Joe 76
BATES, Gen. 69; John 89; Martin 89
BATTLE CREEK 131
BATTLE OF RESACA 18
BAXTER, Judge 51
BAYLESS, Asa 40
BEAGLES, Lt. A.W. 6; Thos. 73,75
BEAVERS, Hiram O. 34,69
BELL, Kale 119
BENSON, John 106; R.W. Samuel 104
BENTON, J.T. 51
BENTONVILLE, NC 27,65,69,75,85
BIG CREEK GAP, TN 10,34,68,75,97,115,119, 123
BIG HILL 8,65,68
BIG SPRING ROAD 62
BIG SPRINGS 13,22,69,99
BIRD, Col. R.K. 19
BIRD'S MILL ROAD 11
BLACK JACK SCHOOL 5
BLACKWELL, Capt. 6; J.L. 129
BLACKSTOCK, Annie 13; Angeline 13; J.C. 12; Mr. 16
BLAIR, Sam 40
BLAKELY, Martha 47
BLEDSOE COUNTY 23,27
BLEVINS, Adjt. Dave 24; Capt. D.C. 45; D.C. 44,61; Dave 55; Dr. A.C. 51; James 35; John 34; Lt. W.F. 84; R.E.L. 52; Rodney 52,55; Ruth (Rockholt) 35; W.F. 32,35, 46,51,64,69; William F. 31
BLOUNT COUNTY, TN 28
BLOUNTVILLE, TN 37,38
BLUE GRASS SECTION, KY 119
BLY, Lt. Jon 80
BLYTHE, Capt. 56; Capt. John 26,59
BLYTHE'S COMPANY 77
BOGOS, Tom 41,44
BOLEN [BOWLING], John 128
BON AIR, White Co., TN 42
BORDEN, Nat 36,40
BOSTON, KY 107,111
BOSWELL BRIDGE 20
BOWLING GREEN, KY 49,50
BRADLEY COUNTY 3,6,29,70,74,75,86,87; Cleveland 6,71; Company 12,27
BRADY, Samuel 29
BRAGG, Gen. 8,10,14,15,34,64,68,69,74,101; Gen. Braxton 131
BRAGG'S ARMY 120
BRANCH, Stephen 125; Tabitha Carson 125; Valencia 125
BRANCHVILLE, SC 26
BREWER, Rev. G.W. 51,97
BRIAR CREEK BATTLE 47
BRIMSTONE, KY 7
BRIMSTONE, TN 39,71,110
BRIMSTONE CREEK 73,75,129
BRISTOL, TN 24,103,104,106,111
BRITTAIN'S COMPANY 86
BRITTEN, Capt. 89
BROOKS, George 128
BROWN, Capt. George 51; Gen. 69; Gov. John C. 50; I.K. 51; Joe 40; William L. 86
BROWN'S COMPANY 86
BROWNLOW, Governor 29; Jim 50
BROXIES, ----- 111
BROYLES, 3rd Lt. Mac B. 39
BRYANT, Jennings 69; William 128
BRYSON, ----- 9
BUCK HEAD CREEK 25
BULL GAP 9,50
BUNKER HILL FERRY 14
BURKE COUNTY, NC 125
BURNSIDES, Gen. 8,10,18
BURSON, John 40
BUSSEL, Cred 76
BUTTRAM CEMETERY 1,31,61
BUZZARD ROOST 39,44
BYBEE, TN 128
BYRNA, Rev. G.D. 111

- C -

CALHOUN, GA 18,34,39
CALHOUN, TN 75
COMBS, Col. 131; Maj. S.H. 131
CAMP, E.S. 9
CAMP CUMMING 120
CAMP DICK ROBERSON 7,9
CAMP MORTON, IND 112
CAMP PINE KNOT, KY 110
CAMPBELL, John 4; Mat [Madison] 40
CAMPBELL COUNTY, TN 39
CANNON, Wm. 40
CANTWELL, David 118; John 118; Perry 116, 118; Thomas 118
CARRIER, TN 111
CARROLL, Gen. 30
CARSON, Jno. 40
CARTER, Ed 70,76; G.W. 111; George 128; John 76
CARTER'S SCOUTS 36,39,40
CARTERS STATION 21
CARTERSVILLE, GA 19,39; Road 19
CASEY, Elizabeth 99; Nancy 99; William 99
CASH, J.A. 51; James A. 46
CASSVILLE, GA 19; Road 19
CATOOSA SPRINGS ROAD 18
CAVE SPRINGS, GA 2,15,68,129
CHAMBERS, Bat 89
CHARLESTON 9,21,26,34,75,88,89
CHARLOTTE, N.C. 2,6,25,27,30,31,34,41,45, 46,50,56,60,61,65,70,74,77,80,81,85,90, 93
CHARLTON, G.W. 37; Joseph Edward 36
CHATTAHOOCHEE RIVER 20
CHATTANOOGA, TN 30,34,47,50,57,59,64, 68,75,84,101,127
CHATTANOOGA ROAD 11,16,68
CHATTIN, Ed 14; J.D. 29
CHEROKEE 50
CHICKAMAUGA, GA 1,6,8,13,19,34,39,44, 50,56,59,64,65,75,84,93,94,97,112,115, 119,123, 127,129,130
CHICKAMAUGA CREEK 12,16; South 10
CHUCKEY KNOB 127
CHURCH OF GOD 45
CLACK, Esqr. Wm 29

CLARK, Barthana 108; James 108
CLARK-DRY FORK CEMETERY 77
CLARKSVILLE, TN 131
CLEBURNE, Gen. 39; Pat 6,17,18
CLEVELAND, TN 14,25,74,75,86,87,89
CLEVELAND ROAD 14,15,18,21
CLIFT, Col. Wm. 9
CLINTON, TN 39,110
COAL'S 54th Virginia 16
COBB, Maj. 10
COCKE COUNTY, TN 107,108,111,113,120, 127
COLLINS, Barbara 30
COLLINSVILLE, ALA 25,94
COLLOM, Jonathan 104; Martha (Serch) 104; Sarah 104
COLSTON, Dave 10
COLUMBIA, SC 25,26
COLUMBIA PIKE 13
COLVILLE, W.E. 5; Will 70,76
COMBS, Lt. Col. 64
COMBS' BATTALION 101
CONCORD 10
CONFEDERATE MONEY 24
CONFEDERATE VETERAN 1,30,46,129,130
CONLEY, Bob 40
COOLEY, G.W. 86; John Franklin 41
COOSA RIVER 25,94
COPELAND, F.M. 111; J.R. 111
CORNERSVILLE, TN 24
CORSE, Gen. 25,94
CORSE'S DIVISION 20
COSBY'S CREEK, Cocke Co., TN 113
COTES, E.B. 115
COTTONPORT, Meigs County, TN 13
COWAN, Mahlon 106
COX'S INFANTRY 20
COX'S DIVISION 19
CRAB ORCHARD 8,68
CRAWFORD, Capt. John 46,47,51; H.A. 51; J.T. 18,130; John 47; John Tyler 46,47; William A. 47
CROSS ROADS [SMITH'S] 44
CROUCH, H. 40; Joe 40
CROW, Sol 84
CROW CREEK 18
CROW VALLEY 18

CROXTON, Lt. 12
CRUTCHFIELD, Wm. 30
CRYSTAL FALLS, TX 50
CULTAN, Will 89
CUMBERLAND COUNTY, TN 80
CUMBERLAND GAP 8,9,10,44,59,61,68,74,
    80,97,106,111,119,123,129
CUMBERLAND MOUNTAIN 44,115,123,127

DOGWOOD VALLEY 12,16
DOSS, Capt. John 50; Mary Kate 50
DUCK RIVER 59,119
DUCKWORTH, D. Frank 56; John 56,60
DUNLAP, TN 13,59,94
DUNN, Hollis 29
DURHAM, J.A. 80
DUVALL, Joe 123

- D -

DAHLONIGA ROAD 18
DALTON, GA 14,18,21,22,25,34,39,44,45,50,
    65,75,93,94,120,130
DALTON ROAD 15,18,21
DANDRIDGE, TN 125,128
DANNIELS, E. 108
DANVILLE, KY 7,129
DANVILLE, VA 25
DARLINGTON 26
DARLINGTON ROAD 26
DARWIN STATION 31
DAVIDSON, Gen. H.B. 15
DAVIS, Bedney 52,55; Ellic [Alex] 73,75; Gen.
    Jeff C. 17; J. Alex 6; Joe 76; John 53;
    President 29, 30; Temmie 52,55; T.A. 52;
    Tennessee A. 52; William Owen 52
DAY, Elbert 119; Jessie 119; S.H. 12; Samuel 73,
    75,103
DAYTON, TN 1,32,34,44,59,62,69,85,87,94,97
DAYTON HERALD 1
DEATHERAGE, William 130
DEBUSK, James 118; Joe 118
DECATUR, ALA 40
DECATUR, TN 41,53,56,61,64,69,85,94,98
DECATUR ACADEMY 33,43
DECATUR ROAD 20,22
DECHERD, TN 23
DELANEY, Dr. 23; Dr. William T. 130; Lieut.
    23; Mrs. Doak Moore 106; Surgeon 12
DELOZIER, Mr. 13
DENTON, Will 128
DETHERAGE, Will 21
DEWITT, 3rd Lt. 111; Alex 128
DIBRELL, Gen. 23,24,26,130
DIVISION, Gen. Humes' 18; Kelly's 18

- E -

EAST TENNESEE FEDERAL TROOPS 19
EAVES, Katherine 85; Thomas 85
EAVES [THOMAS] CEMETERY 81
ETOWAH RIVER 19
EUTAW SPRINGS BATTLE 47
EVANS, ----- 111
EVENSVILLE, TN 31,34
EXCELSIOR SPRINGS, MO 115.123

- F -

FARMINGTON, TN 68,94,112
FAYETTEVILLE 27
FATEVILLE, BEDFORD COUNTY 30
FEDERAL HOSPITAL 12
FEDERAL ROAD 21
FINCASTLE 52
FINE, Vincent 128
FISHING CREEK, KY 59,94,106
FLAT GAP, TN 119
FLEMMING, James 51
FLINT SPRING CEMETERY 86
FLORENCE 26,27
FORMAN, Jack 40
FORREST, Gen. 56,59
FORT DONELSON 47,49,50,123
FORT NELSON 7
FRALY, Jim 29
FRANKLIN 39
FRAZIER, Abner 3; Ann 30; Beriah 30; Capt.
    S.J.A. 13; N.P. 18; Ruth 23
FRAZIER CEMETERY 28
FRAZIER'S BEND 30

FRAZIER'S BRANCH 13
FRAZIER'S FERRY 21
FRENCH BROAD 50,93
FRY, Gen. 7
FUGATE SEVEN 29
FURGUSON, H.L.W. 97

- G -

GADSDEN, ALA 25
GANNAWAY, E.N. 51
GANT, Reeves 123
GARRARD, Gen. 19,20,25
GARRARD'S BRIGADE, 18,19
GARRAWAY, Ephr. 97
GASTON, Wm. 51
GAY STREET (Knoxville) 9
GEORGETOWN 14
GEORGIA — see Adairsville, Athens, Atlanta, Augusta, Calhoun, Cartersville, Cassville, Cave Springs, Chattahoochee River, Chickamauga, Dahloniga Road, Dalton, Etowah River, Graysville, Jonesboro, Kenesaw, Macon, Marietta, Murry County, New Hope Church, Newman, Ocmulgee River, Oostenaula River, Peachtree Battle, Red Clay, Resaca, Ringgold, Rocky Face Mountain, Rome, Roswell Factory, Sand Town, Savannah, Tilton, Trickum, Tunnel Hill, Washington
GIBBONS, John 66; Mary 66
GIBBS, Barbara 30; Lt. 9
GIBSON, Bill 119; Columbus 51; Jos. 40
GILLESPIE, Col. J.W. 6,29,41; Gen. 120; J.W. 77,86,90,103,124; Lt. Hal 11
GODSEY, N.C. 61; Stephen Jett 66; W.C. 34,62; Will 90,97; William Clenton 61,66
GODSEY'S SCHOOL HOUSE 64
GOINS, Col. 30
GOOD HOPE BAPTIST CHURCH 69
GOODFIELD, TN 69
GOODFIELD CREEK 21
GOOSE CREEK 7,8,10
GORMAN, Thomas 124
GORMAN'S COMPANY 124

GRADY, Ben 76
GRAHAM, Capt. 27,116; Capt. John 119
GRAINGER, Gen. 18
GRAINGER COUNTY, TN 47,107,108
GRAVES, J.P. 128; J.R. 69
GRAY, Alex 123
GRAYSVILLE, GA 10,16
GRAYSVILLE ROAD 16
GREEN BACK PARTY 7
GREENSBORO, NC 25,50,101
GREGORY, Eligah 55
GRIFFEN, Francis 123
GRIFFITH, Isaac 70-76,130; Jane Shelton 47; Levi 47; Martha 47
GRIFFITH, NC 97
GROSS, George 21
GUFFEE, A.E. 77; Andy White 77-80; Bill 80; Ephraim 80; Lt. William 130; Rebecca 77
GUFFEY, Carter 59; Jim 59; Sam 59
GUINN, J.D. 73,75; Ord. Sgt. John D. 12
GULLY, James 119
GUM SPRINGS Church 4; School 5
GWINN, Frank 55

- H -

HAIRSTER, P.L. 70,76
HALE, Alf 119; Nancy Jane 102
HAMBLIN COUNTY, TN 108
HAMILTON COUNTY 6,47; Company 12
HAMPTON, Joe 55
HAMILTON'S TENN CAVALRY BAT 131
HANCOCK COUNTY, TN 117,119
HARPER, 1st Lt. G.W. 111; George 128; William 128
HARRIMAN, TN 24
HARRIS, Dick 76; Gov. Isham G. 50,69,89; Tip 97
HARRISON COURTHOUSE 29
HARRODSBURG 8
HART'S 6th GEORGIA 8,11
HARTSELL, David 123
HAWKINS COUNTY, TN 24,66
HAYES, Landon C. 89; Uriah 51
HAYSE, Harmon 119
HAZZARD, KY 9

HAZZARD COUNTY 8
HEADRICKS, ----- 111
HEDRICK, Summerfield 128
HENRY, ---- 111; J.L. 97; Joseph 97; Marshall 128
HICKEY, Adjt. A.C. 46; Austin 123; John 123
HICKMAN, Capt. Edmund 47
HICKORY STATION, N.C. 2
HILL, Gen. J.B. 40
HIWASSEE RIVER 9,10,13,14,21,34,47,68
HOG BACK COMPANY 102
HOGG, Gov. Jas. S. 51
HOLSTON RIVER, 108; South Fork of 24
HOLSTON VALLEY 106
HOOD, Adjt. 50; Gen. 19,20,21,25,36,39,44,85; Tom 59
HOOKER, Gen. 17
HOOPER, Esqr. 4
HOPE, Asa 40
HOPKINS, ----- 111; Baxter 128; Ben 128; Bob 112,115; Gum 124,128; Jasper 115,128; Joseph 112,115
HORN, Uncle Sherd 111
HORNER, Isaac N. 129; Lt. 7,9; Lt. William F. 129
HOWARD, Doc 36,40; George 36; Joseph 36
HOWELL, J.A. 51; John 29; Rachel 29; Tim 31,34
HOYAL, Dr. John 5,28,29
HUFF, Jim 128
HULSE, Bill 40
HUMES, Gen. 15
HUMES' DIVISION 19,20,21,25
HUNTER, Harriet B. (Whitesides) 81; John 85; P.E. 84; Pleas/Pleasant 34,69; Pleasant Eaves 81-85
HUNTER'S BLUFF 22
HUNT'S DIVISION 104
HUTCHINSON, Phillip 23
HUTSELL, Mr. 14

- I -

INDIANAPOLIS, IND 47
IRVINE, KY 130

- J -

JACKSBORO/JACKSBOROUGH 70,97,123
JACKSBURROE 75
JACKSON, Gen. 21,25; Isaac 40
JACKSON COUNTY, ALA 3
JAKES, Capt. 7
JAMESTOWN, TN 123
JEFFERSON COUNTY, TN 85,127
JENNOE, H. 51
JETT, Elizabeth 39
JEWELL, J.H. 51; James 51
JOHNSON, Ace 51; Andrew 50; Andy 69,89; Asa 8,14,97; Bratch 56,59; F.L.B. 56; James 51; Sheriff 47
JOHNSON HOGE SEVEN 29
JOHNSON'S ISLAND, OHIO 98,102
JOHNSTON, Gen. 68,69,94; Gen. J.E. 15,21, 26,30; Jim 89; Joseph E. 85
JONES, B.F. 87; M.V. 86-89; Martin V. 86; W.O. 25,27
JONESBORO, GA 18,20,21,34.68
JONESBORO, TN 24,46,94
JONESBORO COMPANY 25
JULIAN, ---- 16; Julia 16

- K -

KELLY, Nancy 121
KELLY'S DIVISION 19
KENESAW, GA 34
KENNESAW MOUNTAIN 19,44,60
KENTUCKY, 8,9,34,39,61,74,119,129; see also Barberville, Blue Grass Section, Bowling Green, Brimstone, Camp Dick Roberson, Camp Pine Knot, Cumberland Gap, Danville, Fishing Creek, Hazzard, Irvine, Lexington, London, Louisville, Middlesboro, Munsfordville, Paris, Perryville, Richmond, Rock Castle, Scott County, Stanton, Summersett, Williamsburg
KENTUCKY CAMPAIGN 101
KENTUCKY RIVER 8
KEY, Judge D.M. 29,51
KILPATRICK, ----- 18,20; Brigade 25; Gen. 27
KINCAID'S COMPANY 77

KINCER, Andy 40
KINCHELO, Eleye [Eldridge] 40; George 40
KING, Amos 93,95; John 24,40; Jerome 61,69; L.M. 131; Luke 25,69; Luke M.C. 90-94; Ruthie 90; Susan Cowan King 106; Tempa (McDaniel) 95
KINGSTON, TN 39,50,73,74,77,78,97,129
KINGSTON JAIL 30
KINGSTON ROAD 10,19
KINSLEY, J.R. 128
KIRK, Col. 34,65,69; Col. Robert 27
KIUKA TRACE 94
KNOXVILLE, TN 18,21,29,39,44,49,50,64,77, 80,103,106,107,115,120,123,124,127,129
KNOXVILLE COMPANY 11
KOLB'S BATTERY 7
KUHN, Capt. 10
KYLE, Robert 30

- L -

LAMB, Jeff 119
LANGSFORD, Lt. 21
LANGSTON, George 89
LANHAM, Gov. Samuel T. 51
LANIS, James Ed 70,75
LANSFORD, Lt. 12; Lt. M.D. 130
LARKINVILLE, ALA 30
LARMER, E.S. 51
LATHAM, Carter 59; Tom 59
LATROBE, Capt. 13
LAUREL GAP ROAD 10
LAVERGNE, TN 24
LAWRENCEBURG 8,9
LAWSON, Colonel/Callamel 73,75; Jake 73,75; Ken 73,75; Nelson 73,75; R.C. 73,75; Russel 73, 75; Winnie A. 75
LAWSON, MO 123
LEA, Jno. H. 111
LEADBETTER, Col. 129
LEE, Gen. 26
LEET'S SPRINGS 11
LENOIR ROAD 10
LEUTY, Capt. Bert 56

LEWIS, ----- 111; Grundy 128; James 70; Jim 55; John 55; Lt. Col. 15; Maj. 34; Maj. Joel 47; Wash 16
LEWIS' BATTALION, 34
LEWISBURG PIKE 13131
LEXINGTON, KY 39
LEXINGTON, VA 104
LEXINGTON & RICHMOND PIKE 8
LICKSKILLET ROAD 21
LILLARD, Capt. 101; Capt. W.W. 22,26,31,61, 64,81,84, 98,101; Jim 55
LILLARD'S COMPANY 61,81,98
LIMESTONE, TN 24
LIMESTONE DEPOT 39
LINON ROAD 18
LIVINGSTON, TN 111
LOCKE, Col. Matthew 47; Jane 22; Judge Frank 29; Leneas 22; T.J. 22,28
LOCKE'S FERRY 28
LOCKE'S FERRY ROAD 22
LONDON, KY 7,9,115
LONGMIRES, 1st Cpl. Jno.39
LOOKOUT MOUNTAIN 50
LOUDEN/LOUDON, TN 119
LOUDERDALE, James 87; Jane 87
LOUDON BRIDGE 10
LOUISVILLE, KY 30
LOVELL, John 128
LOWE, Samuel 29
LOYD, B.F. 27; John 9,12,13,129,130
LUSK, John 89
LUTHER, TN 117,119

- Mc -

McCLANNAHAN, George 128
McCRARY, Joseph 21
McCONELL, Maj. Tom 24
McCOOK, ----- 18; Gen. 19,20
McCORKLE'S MILL 21,22
McCOY, Wiley 119
McDANIEL, Samuel 93,95; Tempa 93,95
McDONALD, Captain Mary 30
McDONALD STATION 14
McDOWELL COUNTY, NC 125

McGAVIN, Col. 21
McGUFFEE, Lt. 18
McGUIRE, Bob 40
McKENZIE, B.G. 102; Benjamin Franklin 99; Capt. 52; Capt. G.W. 6; Col. 8,9,10,11, 12,15,17,19,21,27,28,50,65,119,123, 124,129; Col. G.W. 15,34,45,62,84,94,98, 101,104; Col. George W. 6,61,99; Dr. J.R. 102; E.G. 41; G.A. 102; G.W. 111; Green 41,44; J.M. 64,69,80,99,131; Jeremiah M. 98-102,130; Jerry M. 34; Lt. J.M. 21,22; Lt. Jerry 84; Lt. Col. 41,44; L.T. 102; Nancy Jane 102
McKENZIE CEMETERY 98
McKENZIE'S 5th Regiment 1; 5th Tennessee 8
McKINSEY, Colonel 73
McLAWS, Gen. 19,26
McLAW'S BRIGADE 19
McLIN, Capt. Jno. B. 39; Col. 44,52,107; Hunter 40; Maj. 25
McLIN'S CAVALRY 36
McLIN'S COMPANY 103
McMAHAN, ----- 111; Dave 76; Eli 113; Miss Didy 113
McMILLEN, Harrison 34
McMINNVILLE, TN 59
McNABB, R.A. 111; Russell 128

- M -

MACON, GA 21,25,68,129
MAJORS, John 51
MARIETTA, GA 19,39
MARION, NC 125
MARTIN, Gen. 18; Jesse 64; Lt. Jess 84; W.O. 44
MARTIN, SC 27
MARTIN'S ACADEMY 105
MARYVILLE 9,28,50
MASONER, Isaac 102; Margaret 102
MATHIS SHOAL 13
MAYNARD, Horace 51
MAYSVILLE RAILROAD 8

MEIGS COUNTY 13,32,34,35,41,42,53,61,62, 81,83,84,90,93,94,95,97,98,99,101,102; see also Bunker Hill Ferry, Cottonport, Decatur, Decatur Academy, Georgetown, Godsey's School House, Goodfield, Hiwassee River, Hunter's Bluff, Locke's Ferry, Pineland, Shiloh Church, Ten Mile
MELTON, W.M. 97
MEXICAN WAR 22,99,101
MIDDLESBORO, KY 10
MIDWAY, TN 36,39
MILIGAN, Luisa 119; Sollomon 119
MILL BRIDGE 19
MILLIGAN, John 40
MIMMS/MIMS, Capt. 129; Capt. A.L. 7,107, 111,112,120,123,128; Capt. Lem 128
MIMMS' SCHOOL 7
MISSION RIDGE 14,39,68
MISSIONARY BAPTIST CHURCH 74,127
MISSIONARY RIDGE 50,59,60
MISSISSIPPIANS, Gen. Ferguson's 20
MOLTON, Nute 61,69
MONTEREY, TN 108,111
MONTGOMERY, Capt. J.G.M. 6,73,75; Col. 15; J.G.M. 70; John George Morgan 3,6; Lt. Col. 10,18,19,119; Sam 76
MOORE, Daniel 104; Ebenezer Melvin Patten 103-106; James 104; John Trotwood 1,27
MORELL, Joe 115
MORELOCK, ----- 111
MORGAN, ----- 119; Gen. 8; Gen. George W. 129; Gen. John H. 8,129
MORGAN COUNTY, TN 39,129
MORRISON, Col. 41; J.B. 80
MORRISTOWN. TN 108,109,128
MORRISTOWN ACADEMY 109
MORTON, Dr. 120
MULLENDORE. Capt. W.W. 39
MULLENDORE'S COMPANY 36,103
MUNSFORDVILLE, KY 34
MURFREESBORO, TN 23,50,61,68,94,123
MURPHY, NC 9,130; jail 9
MURRY COUNTY, GA. 18,130
MUSCLE SHOALS 59
MYERS, J.E. 40

- N -

NANCE, ----- 55; J.C. 52
NASHVILLE, TN 7,30,123
NATURAL BRIDGE, VA 104
NEAL, Col. J.R. 8; Thomas 61,69
NELSON, Greenbury 76; Tom 24
NETT, Dec 111
NEW HOPE BATTLE 19
NEW HOPE BRIDGE 6
NEW HOPE CHURCH, GA 34,60,64,85,119
NEW ORLEANS 47
NEWMAN, GA 20
NEWPORT, TN 112,115,120,121,127,128
NICKAJACK 20
NORTH CAROLINA 93; see also Ashville, Bentonville, Burke County, Charlotte, Greensboro, Griffith, Hickory Station, McDowell County, Marion, Murphy, Raleigh, Surry County
NORTH CHATTANOOGA, TN 69
NORTH HOLSTON RIVER 47

- O -

OCMULGEE RIVER 21
OHIO 8
OHIO RIVER 30
OOSTENAULA RIVER 18
ORANGE RIVER 26
ORCHARD KNOB 10,34,68
ORR, Capt. John M. 106
OVERTON COUNTY, TN 108,110
OWENS, Capt. 11; John 55

- P -

PACK MILL ROAD 19
PAINE, Hanibal 29,51; Maj. F.J. 29
PALMER, General 30,123
PAMPA, Gray County, TX 50
PAREGON, Henry 111
PARIS, KY 8,39,68,80
PARKS, Cal 76; Wash 76
PEACHTREE BATTLE 60
PEARSON, Jos. 59
PEATERS, Ad 119
PEAVINE CREEK 11
PEEDEE RIVER 27
PEGRAM, Gen. John 7,129
PEGRAM'S BRIGADE 104
PEOPLE'S COLLEGE 23
PERRYVILLE, KY 8,9,34,61,64,68,74,80,97, 101
PERRYVILLE BATTLE 34,44
PHAR SEVEN, WILLIAM 29
PHILADELPHIA, TN 75,104
PHILADELPHIA PIKE 10
PICKETT MILL 6
PIKEVILLE, TN 23,27
PINELAND, Meigs Co. TN 69
POINT LOOKOUT, MD 112
POLK, Gen. 19; Hanse 70,75; James K. 89
POOR, Ike 40
PORTER, James 89
POWDER SPRINGS ROAD 6,19
POWELL, T.B. 69
PRIGMORE, Thomas 28
PUTMAN, John 76
PUTNAM COUNTY, TN 110

- R -

RACCOON FORD 19
RAGAN, Capt. Jack 12,26,27
RAINS, John D. 29,131
RALEIGH, NC 25,97
RAMSEY CEMETERY 70
RANKIN, TN 128
RAY [RHEA], J.H. 110; Wm. 40
RAY COUNTY, MO 123
REAGAN, Capt. 130
RED BANK, TN 69
RED CLAY, GA 14
REDDERICK, W.S. 15
REED'S BRIDGE 11
RESACA BATTLE 27,34
RESACA, GA 18,39,44,60

REVOLUTIONARY WAR 47,99
RHEA COUNTY 11,14,18,30,47,47,48,57,66; see also Black Jack School, Dayton, Frazier's Bend, Gum Springs, Kiuka Trace, Rhea Springs, Smith's Cross Roads, Spring City, Sulphur Springs, Washington, Washington Academy
RHEA SPRINGS, TN 56
RICEVILLE, TN 21
RICHARDSON, A. 3
RICHMAN 75
RICHMOND 8
RICHMOND, KY 39,68,80,119
RICHMOND, MO 123
RICHMOND, VA 24,37,115
RICHMOND BATTLE 65
RINGGOLD, GA 12,34,119,130
RINGGOLD GAP 10,11
RINGGOLD ROAD 11,68
RINGO, Billy 123
ROANE COUNTY, TN 30,78,80,
ROANOKE, VA 16
ROBERSON, Camp Dick 7; Gen. 26,27
ROBERTSON, Gen. Felix 23,24,130
ROBINSON, T.J. 51
ROCKBRIDGE COUNTY, VA 104
ROCK CASTLE, KY 9
ROCKHOLT, Frank 35; Ruth 35
ROCKY FACE MOUNTAIN 16,17,18
ROCK ISLAND BARRACKS, ILL 130
RODDY, George P. 51
ROGERS, J.F. 2
ROGERSVILLE, TN 24,50
ROGGERS, Col. John 89
ROME, GA 18
RORSE [ROSE], John 76
ROSECRANS, wagon train 13,94
ROSE'S FURNACE 107
ROSS' LANDING 47
ROSWELL FACTORY 20
RUNIONS, William 11
RUSSELL, Cog 70,76; Maj. William 14; Mary E. 31; Miss Sarah 14; Tallor 70,76
RUTHERFORD, Col. 47; Joseph 128
RUTLEDGE'S (R.A.) COMPANY 86

- S -

SALEM CHURCH 104
SALTVILLE, VA 24,130
SAMPSON, Isaac 40
SANTA ANNA 101
SAND TOWN, GA 20
SANDER'S RAID 130
SAUNDERS, C.W. 51
SAVANNAH, GA 65,75,84,85
SAVANNAH RIVER 26,69,75,85
SCOTT, Col. 11,15,80; Col. John S. 8,10,64; Gen. 101
SCOTT COUNTY, KY 64
SCOTT COUNTY, TN 71,75,110,129
SCOTT COUNTY, VA 66
SCOTT'S 1st Louisiana 11; 1st Louisiana Tigers 7
SCOTT'S RAID 129,130
SCOTT'S WAR (FLORIDA INDIANS) 30
SEHON, John F. 107-111; W.G. 108
SEQUATCHIE VALLEY 13,68,75,94
SERCH, Martha 104
SEVEN NOTCH ROAD 26
SEVIERVILLE, TN 50
SHARP, Jno. 111
SHAW, Lt. Col. 26
SHEFIELD, Jim 40
SHELBYVILLE 112
SHELTON, Huston 123
SHERMAN, Gen. 15,18,69,75; Gen. W.T. 30
SHERMAN'S CAVALRY 25,27
SHERMAN'S SUPPLY TRAIN 19
SHEMAN'S INFANTRY 21
SHILOH CHURCH 21,22,31,34,61,68,81,84,98,101
SHUGART, Will 86,89
SICKAMORE SHOALS, TN 34
SIMSON [SIMPSON], Bob 76
SISK, Polly 121; Tolliver 121
SLOAN, Dr. Felix 73,75; Flavis 76; Lt. R.F. 6; Robbert 73,75; Robert 129; William B. 129,130
SMIDLY [SMEDLEY], Bill 76

SMITH, Andy 80; Capt. 47; Geo. 40; J.C. 26; Margaret 80; S.A. 86; Sgt. T.H. 84; Tom 59,69; Thomas 69
SMITH'S FERRY 28
SMITH'S X ROADS, Rhea County 13,29,39,59, 93,94,97; see also Dayton
SNAKE CREEK GAP 18
SNEEDVILLE, TN 116
SNOW, Larkin 60; Rebecca 60
SOUTH CAROLINA 45; see also Branchville, Columbia, Martin
SPARTA, TN 34,64,101,131
SPEARS, Joe 76
SPENCE, C.D. 119
SPRADLING, Eliza Louise 52
SPRING CITY, TN 97
SPRINGVILLE 19
STANFORD 8
STANLEY, Alfred 36; Isaac 36,40
STANTON, KY 8,27,68
STAR ROUTE 62
STAUNTON, VA 47
STEEDMAN, Gen. 30
STEPHENS, Bob 39; Bugler Bill M. 39
STEWART, Capt. George 120; John 14
STOKELY, Dave 128; Elisha 128; Will 128
STOKES, Col. Bill 23
STOKLIE, ----- 111
STONEMAN, Gen. 19
STOVER, John 29
STRANGE, Bill 128
STRAWBERRY PLAINS 106
SULLIVAN COUNTY, TN 36,37,106
SULLIVAN'S FERRY 14
SULPHUR SPRINGS, TN 56
SUMMERSETT, KY 7,9
SUNDAY, Billy 69
SURRY COUNTY, NC 47
SUTTON, John 76
SWAFFORD, Aaron 23
SWANN, Col. A.R. 128
SWAN POND 106
SWEETWATER, TN 22,28; Valley 28
SYCAMORE SHOALS 8

- T -

TAFF, John 84
TALBOT, Jefferson Co., TN 37
TALLEY, Asberry 130; Berry 21
TARTER, Harve 119
TASWELL 74
TAYLOR, Gov. Alf 50; Greenfield 119; Henry H. 36,40; Robert L. 50,89,128; Tip 36,40
TAZEWELL, TN 106
TEN MILE, Meigs County, TN 14
TENNESSEE — see Altamont, Athens, Big Creek Gap, Bledsoe County, Blount County, Blountville, Bon Air, Bradley County, Brimstone, Bristol, Bybee, Calhoun, Campbell County, Carrier, Chattanooga, Clarksville, Cleveland, Clinton, Cocke County, Cornersville, Cosby's Creek, Cottonport, Cumberland County, Dandridge, Dayton, Decatur, Decherd, Dunlap, Evensville, Farmington, Flat Gap, Goodfield, Grainger County, Hamblin County, Hamilton County, Hancock County, Harriman, Hawkins County, Hiwassee River, Jamestown, Jefferson County, Jonesboro, Kingston, Knoxville, Lavergne, Limestone, Livingston, Lookout Mountain, Louden/ Loudon, Luther, McMinnville, Meigs County, Mission / Missionary Ridge, Monterey, Morgan County, Morristown, Murfreesboro, Nashville,. Newport, North Chattanooga, Orchard Knob, Overton County, Philadelphia, Pikeville, Pineland, Putnam County, Rankin, Red Bank, Rhea County, Rhea Springs, Riceville, Roane County, Rogersville, Scott County, Sequatchie County, Sevierville, Shelbyville, Sickamore Shoals, Smith's X Roads, Sneedville, Sparta, Spring City, Sullivan County, Sulphur Springs, Sweetwater, Talbot, Tazewell, Treadway, Washington, Washington County, White County, Winchester
TENNESSEE RIVER 22,28,62,68,84
TERHUNE, A.C. 129
TEXAS RANGERS 107,111

THOMAS, Gen. 17,40
THOMISON, Lizzie 16; Mary E. 4; W.P. 51,97
THOMPSON, J.M. 28
TILTON, GA 6,18,21
TIPTON, Elizabeth 37; John 37
TODD, G.R. 51; George 29; J.M. 25; John 84
TOW STRING CREEK 19
TREADWAY, TN 119
TRICKUM, GA 16
TUCKER, George 76; Jo 14; John 89
TULLAHOMA 46,50
TUNNEL HILL, GA 11,15,16,18,21,26,31,34, 36,41,44,56,61,68,77,81,90,93,98,107, 112,116,119,120,124,130
TYLER, TX 47

- V -

VAUGHN, Gen. 75; Gen. J.C. 24; Gen. John C. 130
VAUGHN'S CAVALRY 50
VAUGHN'S DIVISION 24
VAUGHN'S 3rd TENN. INFANTRY 129
VIRGINIA — see Abington, Coal's, Danville, Lexington, Natural Bridge, Richmond, Rockbridge County, Saltville, Scott County, Staunton
VIRGINIA SALT WORKS 24

- W -

WAID [WADE], Jared 76
WALDEN'S RIDGE 22,59
WALKER, J.P. 29; Jo 70,76; John P. 30; Peet 119; Seth 76; Silvester 119
WALLS, W.E. 17
WALNUT GROVE CEMETERY 52
WAR CREEK 119
WARREN, Jim 76
WARTBURG 75
WASHINGTON ACADEMY 5,49
WASHINGTON, GA 30

WASHINGTON, Rhea County, TN 2,3,13,16, 22,23,25,28,29,46,47,49,69,94
WASHINGTON COLLEGE 104
WASHINGTON COUNTY, TN 47,103,104
WATAUGA RIVER 28
WATERHOUSE'S COMPANY 30
WAUTAUGAH VALLEY 65
WAYNESBORO, GA 119
WEATHERFORD, TX 50
WELCH, James 128
WELKER'S BATTALION 30
WESTERN & ATLANTIC RAILROAD 10, 16,18
WESTMORELAND, Henry 89
WHARTON, Gen. 8
WHEELER, Gen. 19,21,24,25,68,69,75,94; Gen. Joe 11,65; Col. James T. 15,17
WHEELER'S Cavalry 50; Corps 19; first Tennessee raid 1,112; Gen. 13,17,24,26; Gen. Joe 50,59; Gen. Joseph 6; Miss Lucy 17; Scouts 36; second Tennessee raid 1,119
WHEELOCK, Boyd 36,40; Peyton B. 36
WHITE, Lt. Col. 129
WHITE COUNTY, TN 42,45
WHITE OAK MOUNTAIN 10,16
WHITE'S CREEK 22
WHITESIDES, Tom 22
WHITSON, Eli 115; James 115; Steve 115; William Maning 112-115
WHITTLE, Ark 51
WILCOX, 2nd Lt. Wash 39
WILDER, Chas. 118; David 118; Gen. 10,34; James 118; Shade 118; Thomas 118; Wiley 118
WILDER'S BRIGADE 11
WILHOIT, Mr. 29
WILLIAMS, ----- 111; Gen. 23,24,25,130; Shelby 8,11
WILLIAMS' KENTUCKY BRIGADE 23
WILLIAMSBURG, KY 7,9,129
WILLIAMSBURG ROAD 10
WILLIS, John 76
WILLS, Jim 70,76
WILSON, ---- 26; Capt. J.C. 28; Gen. 26; Lt. Sam 12,16; Orderly Sgt. D.R. 39; Woods 11
WINCHESTER, TN 23

WINCHESTER PIKE 8
WOLF, Nick 119
WOLFE, George 119; John 116-119
WOOD/WOODS, Ben 112,115; Gipson 121; James 115; Toliver 120-123,128
WOODY, William Jefferson 124-128; William Tate 125
WOOLRIGHT, Capt. Gibson 47

WORK, Val 51; Wm. 51
WRIGHT, Lt. W.W. 46

- Z -

ZOLLICOFFER 106